Voices of Freedom
Harriet Tubman, Sojourner Truth, and Other Women Abolitionists Who Shattered Chains
Elise Baker

© **Copyright 2023 - All rights reserved.**

The content contained within this book may not be reproduced, duplicated or transmitted without direct written permission from the author or the publisher.

Under no circumstances will any blame or legal responsibility be held against the publisher, or author, for any damages, reparation, or monetary loss due to the information contained within this book, either directly or indirectly.

Legal Notice:

This book is copyright protected. It is only for personal use. You cannot amend, distribute, sell, use, quote or paraphrase any part, or the content within this book, without the consent of the author or publisher.

Disclaimer Notice:

Please note the information contained within this document is for educational and entertainment purposes only. All effort has been executed to present accurate, up to date, reliable, complete information. No warranties of any kind are declared or implied. Readers acknowledge that the author is not engaged in the rendering of legal, financial, medical or professional advice. The content within this book has been derived from various sources. Please consult a licensed professional before attempting any techniques outlined in this book.

By reading this document, the reader agrees that under no circumstances is the author responsible for any losses, direct or indirect, that are incurred as a result of the use of the information contained within this document, including, but not limited to, errors, omissions, or inaccuracies.

Contents

Introduction   VI
    Background
    Our Six Women
    Other Factors to Consider

1. Harriet Tubman   1
    The Moses of Her People
       Childhood and Early Life
       Significant Events
       Early Adulthood and Escape
       The Underground Railroad
       Espionage
       Later Years
       Harriet's Cultural Legacy

2. The Grimké Sisters   22
    Trailblazers of Activism
       Upbringing and Awakening
       Defying Social Norms
       Challenging the Status Quo

    Silencing the Sisters

    The Sisters' Cultural Legacy

3. Sojourner Truth   45

   The Unwavering Truth Seeker

    Early Life and Escape from Slavery

    Speeches and Advocacy for Abolition

    Intersectionality: Her Fight for Women's Rights and Abolition

    Later Life

    Truth's Cultural Legacy

4. Elizabeth Heyrick   66

   Mother of Immediatism

    Early Life

    Role in the British Abolitionist Movement

    "Immediate, Not Gradual Abolition"

    Collaboration with American Abolitionists

    Lasting Impact

5. Mary Ann Shadd Cary   89

   Champion of Change

    Safe Haven

    Opening the Door

    On the Fringe

    Lady Lawyer's Legacy

6. Conclusion   110
   Uniting Voices
       Summary

About the Author   120

Also By   122

References & Bibliography   125

Introduction

In this book, we look at the lives of six extraordinary women who all, in their own way, fought against the oppression and shackles of slavery. Traditionally, women's voices have been excluded from the history of slavery and its abolition. Why are there so few accounts of women and the role they played in this period of history? They were silenced and rendered invisible back then—why are they still absent from history books today?

The names of male abolitionists such as William Wilberforce and Thomas Clarkson are well-remembered for their part in the movement to end Britain's involvement in the slave trade, but the names of their female counterparts have been wiped from popular memory (Milmo, 2015). This is because, in the past, history has focused almost exclusively on the lives of men. As well as this, in the 18th and 19th centuries, women were deprived of the vote and had no other form of direct political power. Instead, they had to fight slavery using indirect tactics, such as writing or lobbying. The private nature of such campaigning meant that it was less likely to be remembered. The role of women in the abolition of slavery is beginning to be recognized, but due to the historic neglect of the involvement of women in the abolition movement, it is yet to be widely understood.

This book will help to redress the balance by profiling six remarkable women who protested against slavery, putting this period of history into its historical and political context, one that includes the Industrial Revolution and the American Civil War. Most significantly, though, the book introduces the reader to six remarkable women who, despite the many challenges they faced, made significant contributions to the abolitionist movement and the fight for women's rights, chiefly in America, and draws parallels to similar industrialized countries such as Canada and Britain. It will highlight their individual stories and accomplishments, as well as how their work intersected and influenced each other.

Between 1662 and 1807, a recorded 3.4 million slaves were transported by British and colonial vessels across the Atlantic Ocean. The slave trade was highly lucrative for those involved in it, which included merchants and plantation owners as well as many middle-class Britons, from small manufacturers to clergymen, who owned several slaves as this was a common form of investment at the time.

The women who actively opposed slavery often did so because they had been slaves themselves or, alternatively, they were horrified by the reports of the suffering slaves experienced in the New World. An expert on the role of women in the abolition movement, Professor Clare Midgley of Sheffield Hallam University, states:

> [The abolitionist] Mary Prince wasn't just telling an individual story—she kept pointing out how this was typical of women's oppression, sexual abuse, physical violence, overwork. This was a very powerful tool that women took up and circulated to promote the campaign. (Mimo, 2015, p. 1)

It is unsurprising that many free women identified with slaves. In the 18th and 19th centuries, women had very few rights. They could not hold office or vote, and before she was married, a woman was under the care of her father with her legal rights transferred to her husband after marriage (if, indeed, she did get married). It is also apparent that the contributions of female abolitionists were not valued by their male contemporaries. For example, wealthy Member of Parliament and evangelical Christian William Wilberforce said:

> For ladies to meet, to publish, to go from house to house stirring up petitions, these appear to me unsuited to the female character as delineated in scripture. (Historic England, 2015, p. 1)

This quote from Wilberforce suggests that many men

did not believe women had a place in the abolition movement. As a bulwark of the abolitionist movement, Wilberforce represented the privileges of the English ruling classes and used his social standing to speak up for the rights of the enslaved and to silence the voices of women. Speaking in public was considered to be unwomanly behavior, as women were expected to be passive, not active, citizens. This worldview and attitude were typical for the time, but it is disappointing that he dismissed and overlooked the outstanding potential of women campaigners for the abolitionist movement.

Are you tired of the lack of recognition and invisibility of women in history? This book acts as a guide to this period of history, to unearth and bring to light the true stories of the heroines of this era. Some are better known than others, but by the end, you will know the names of these women and why they should be remembered today. If you are interested in female empowerment, you will love reading these true stories about women whose achievements are not widely known.

Background

The slave trade was established in the mid-17th century and persisted into the 19th century. The slave trade involved exchange of people and goods between Africa, Europe, and the Americas. Ships traveled from Europe full of manufactured goods and then sailed to the West

Coast of Africa, where these goods were traded for people captured by African traders. When the ship was full of people, it would depart for the Americas or the Caribbean. It would then embark on the notorious Middle Passage. During this voyage, the slaves would be kept in the ship's hold, crammed close together with little or no space to move. Male captives were generally chained together to save space, while women and children were given slightly more room. Conditions were unbearable and many people died during the voyage. Close quarters facilitated the spread of disease and, as crew generally did not visit the hold in which the slaves were kept, many of the living enslaved could find themselves shackled to a dead body for hours or even days at a time. Estimates as to the number of people enslaved through these means vary. It has been estimated that by the 1790s, there were 480,000 people enslaved in the British colonies (The British Library, 2023). In other accounts, various historians estimate that between 9.4 and 12.6 million Africans embarked on the voyage to the New World and a life of slavery (Davidson, 1961; Elitis & Richardson, 2002).

Once the enslaved people had been sold in the Americas or the Caribbean, the final leg of the voyage was the return home to Europe where the ships were filled with cargos of sugar, rum, tobacco, and other luxury items. The majority of these enslaved people came to work on plantations in the Americas and the Caribbean that produced tobacco and sugar that would be sold to Europe.

The movement to end slavery was known as "the abolition" or "the abolitionist movement." It began in the 18th century when both the English and American Quakers raised questions about the morality of slavery. This movement was not confined to the United States as powerful voices against slavery also emerged in Britain and Canada. One of the earliest examples of abolitionist activity occurred in the colony of Georgia in 1735 when its governor, James Oglethorpe, influenced by Enlightenment thought, banned slavery and rum. Another pivotal case that led to the emergence of the abolitionist movement was the Somerset Case that took place in 1772, where a fugitive slave was freed on the basis of the judgment that slavery did not exist under English common law. However, the abolition movement in America really began to pick up steam after the American Revolution and the foundation of the United States. For example, many Loyalists fled the Northern United States and settled in the British province of Quebec in modern-day Canada, bringing their slaves with them. This led Quebec to ban slavery in 1793. Abolitionism was also popular in the Northern states of the United States during the same period as, beginning with Pennsylvania in 1780, several Northern states passed legislation to abolish slavery between that point and 1800, sometimes by gradual emancipation.

The tide of public opinion was turning. People in industrialized nations began to raise their voices in protest at the inhumane treatment of fellow human beings. In

Britain, the Clapham Sect was formed in 1785 to fight against slavery and promote other social reforms. Furthermore, in 1787, the Society of Effecting the Abolition of the Slave Trade was formed in London. The society became the first fully developed pressure group and would ultimately succeed in bringing about the abolition of the transatlantic slave trade. An act was passed in Parliament in 1807 that abolished the slave trade throughout the British Empire. However, slavery persisted in the British colonies until its final abolition in 1838. Also, abolitionists continued to campaign against the international trade of slaves long after that date. Slavery was not entirely abolished in the United States until the passing of the 13th Amendment by Congress, which was passed on January 31, 1865, and ratified on December 6, 1865. This meant that slavery was finally outlawed by the United States constitution.

Our Six Women

The six women who played core parts in the abolitionist movement that will be explored in-depth in this book are introduced below.

Harriet Tubman (1822–1913)

Born Araminta Ross, Harriet was an American social activist and abolitionist. After she escaped from slavery, she completed an estimated 19 missions that resulted in the rescue of around 300 enslaved people, including some of her own family and friends, as part of the network of anti-slavery activists and safehouses dubbed the Underground Railroad. Later on in life, Harriet was an activist in the women's suffrage movement.

The Grimké Sisters

Sarah Moore Grimké (1792–1873) and **Angelina Emily Grimké (1805–1879)** were the first white American female campaigners for the abolition of slavery and women's rights to become famous across the United States. The sisters grew up in a slave-owning family in South Carolina, but in the 1820s Sarah and Angelina moved to Philadelphia and joined the city's influential Quaker Society. From then on, they became deeply involved in the abolitionist movement, traveling on the lecture circuit and retelling their firsthand experience of slavery on their family plantation. Because Sarah and Angelina were among the first American women to act publicly in the social reform movement, they received a great deal of ridicule for their abolitionist activity. Nevertheless, the sisters were instrumental members of the abolitionist campaign in the early 19th century.

Sojourner Truth (c. 1797–1883)

Born into slavery as Isabella Baumfree in Swartekill, New York, Sojourner Truth escaped to freedom with her infant daughter in 1826. However, she was unable to take any of her other children to freedom with her, which led her to be the first Black woman to win a case against a White man when she took Solomon Gedney to court to reclaim her son Peter in 1828. Isabella rechristened herself "Sojourner Truth" in 1843 after she became convinced that God had told her to leave the city and live in the countryside, "testifying to the hope that was in her" (Robertson, 2011, p. 91). This was the revelation that led her to speak publicly about her experiences of slavery as part of the abolitionist cause.

Elizabeth Heyrick (1769–1831)

Elizabeth Heyrick is the only British woman explored in this book. Born Elizabeth Coltman, she married lawyer John Heyrick in 1787. Following his death in 1795, she became a Quaker and a social reformer. As part of her involvement in the abolitionist movement, Elizabeth produced leaflets and took up lobbying, encouraging grocers in the Midlands not to stock slave-grown goods as part of a more radical strategy against slavery. In 1824, Elizabeth published an anonymous pamphlet that called for slavery to end immediately, challenging the gradual approach promoted by contemporary campaigners such as William Wilberforce and his supporters. She was also a skilled politician, proposing that the increasing number of female anti-slavery organizations should withhold their donations unless the gradualist approach was abandoned, with theirs representing 20% of overall donations to abolitionist organizations (Milmo, 2015). However, Elizabeth died in 1831, which meant she did not live to see the passing of the Slavery Abolition Act in 1833.

Mary Ann Camberton Shadd Cary (1823–1893)

Born Mary Ann Shadd in Wilmington, Delaware to free African Americans, Mary Ann would grow up to become an American-Canadian anti-slavery activist, teacher, journalist, publisher, and lawyer. Her family was actively involved in the Underground Railroad, assisting those that wished to flee slavery. Her abolitionist activism was mainly associated with her publishing activity, which began in 1849 with a letter published in Frederick Douglass's *North Star* newspaper and a pamphlet entitled *Hints to the Colored People of the North*. In 1853, Mary Ann would go on to found an anti-slavery newspaper, *The Provincial Freeman*. The newspaper was "devoted to anti-slavery, temperance, and general literature," published weekly, and ran for four years before it was forced to fold due to financial problems (Ramon, 2021, p. 35). Despite experiencing considerable criticism due to her gender and political involvement, Mary Ann would continue to seek leadership in Black civil rights organizations.

Other Factors to Consider

Many other factors also impacted on the abolitionist cause and the behavior of female abolitionists during the period, some of which are explored below. The Industrial Revolution that began in the mid-18th century brought about great changes in economic and social organization across the United States, Canada, and Great Britain, such as increased international trade and a wider distribution of wealth. As well as this, previously agrarian societies were transformed into urban, industrialized cities. Other than working-class women being used as a source of cheap factory labor, women were not allowed to play an active part in the Industrial Revolution. Victorian ideas of gender dictated that men and women belonged in "separate spheres," with women being physically weaker yet morally superior to men and therefore suited to the domestic sphere rather than public life (Hughes, 2014). This view of womanhood was heavily promoted by evangelicals. It was yet another way of denying women a voice, disguised as chivalry.

On the other hand, religious commentators in the 19th century tended to promote a more tolerant view toward race. For example, Oxford University's Regius Professor of Modern History, Thomas Arnold, commented that "the mixture of races is essential to the improvement of mankind" (Kirby, 2016, p. 50). Such views challenged notions of eugenics, which became increasingly popular as the 19th century wore on. Thus, while religion rendered women second-class citizens, it promoted surprisingly positive views about race.

One pivotal point in the abolitionist narrative was the end of the American Civil War in 1865. This event led to the creation of the single political entity of the United States and the freedom of over four million enslaved Americans. However, the end of slavery did not represent the end of the oppression of Black people in the United States. After slavery had legally come to an end, state governments across the Southern states introduced laws known as the "Black Codes," which granted certain legal rights to Black people, such as marriage, ownership of property, and the right to sue in court. On the other hand, the Black Codes also made it illegal for Black people to serve on juries, serve in state militias, and testify against White people. Black people also continued to live in extreme poverty. Hence, the abolition of slavery did not mean the end of suffering or the beginning of prosperity for many former slaves.

Another major population shift in the United States in the 19th century took place due to immigration, with nearly 12 million immigrants arriving in the country between 1870 and 1900 (Library of Congress, 2023). Immigrants to the United States also expressed mixed attitudes toward abolition. While many poorer migrants opposed abolition on the basis that former slaves would be competing with them for jobs, others supported the cause because they believed they had common class interests with slaves.

Many of the women involved in the abolitionist movement, such as Harriet Tubman and the Grimké sisters, later became involved in the women's suffrage movement. Within the abolitionist movement, women began to engage publicly, and this naturally led to the promotion of women's rights within the movement, even by like-minded abolitionist men such as Frederick Douglass and William Lloyd Garrison. While many of the women studied in this book, including Harriet Tubman, Sojourner Truth, and Mary Ann Shadd Cary were either born into slavery or were the descendants of slaves, others like the Grimké sisters and Elizabeth Heyrick were wealthy women who carried out "charitable good works" on the behalf of the poor. In some cases, the wealthy women involved in such "good works" did so believing that the uneducated poor and working classes were incapable of representing themselves. It will therefore be important to consider this view when examining the lives and achievements of our women.

Most of the women studied here also had links to two of the most prominent American feminists of the 19th century, Susan B. Anthony and Elizabeth Cady Stanton. Susan B. Anthony (1820–1906) was an American social reformer and women's rights activist. In 1851, she met her lifelong friend Elizabeth Cady Stanton (1815–1902) who became her co-worker in social reform activities, particularly in the field of women's rights. In 1868, the two women began a newspaper called *The Revolution* in which they actively campaigned for women's rights. Both women also had links to the temperance and abolition movements. It was through their work in these areas that Anthony and Stanton established links with all of our women apart from Elizabeth Heyrick.

Harriet Tubman met Anthony when she lived in New York and was encouraged by her to settle in Lake Erie, Canada in the early 1850s. Meanwhile, the Grimké sisters were family friends with Stanton and Sarah was invited by the former to attend the first women's rights convention at Seneca Falls, New York in 1848. Also, both Sojourner Truth and Mary Ann Shadd Cary worked alongside Anthony and Stanton as part of their women's suffrage campaigning in the 1860s and 1870s. Alongside Anthony, Mary Ann adopted a strategy of attempting to register to vote and showing up at polls in the 1870s, while Truth broke ranks with Anthony and Stanton in the 1860s when Stanton stated that she would not support the Black vote if women were not also given the right. These examples emphasize the many links between our six women and Anthony and Stanton and the role these other remarkable women played in their stories.

Chapter One
Harriet Tubman
The Moses of Her People

Harriet Tubman is possibly the most famous of the powerful, influential, and courageous women we will encounter. This chapter chronicles her remarkable journey. Below, we examine the life of Harriet Tubman, an escaped slave who became a conductor on the Underground Railroad and helped 300 enslaved people find freedom. The following sections discuss her journey from captive to liberator: her childhood, her escape from slavery, her work as a conductor, as well as her later charitable and philanthropic activities.

Childhood and Early Life

Harriet Tubman was born Araminta "Minty" Ross to Harriet "Rit" Green and Ben Ross, both of whom were slaves. Like many enslaved people, the time and place of Harriet's birth are unknown or uncertain. Harriet herself later said that she had been born in 1825, her death certificate says 1815, and her gravestone 1820. However, research by historian Kate Larson narrowed the year of her birth down to 1822 based on a payment made to a midwife and several other historical documents, including her runaway advertisement (Larson, 2004). Based on these discoveries, more recent biographies accept March 1822 as Harriet's most likely date of birth (Oertel, 2016; Dunbar, 2019; Walters, 2020).

There is little information available about Harriet's ancestry, although her maternal grandmother, Modesty, is known to have arrived in the United States on a slave ship from Africa. Also, her mother may have had a White father and, as a child, Harriet was told that she seemed like an Ashanti person due to her character traits, although no evidence has been found to prove any Ashanti ancestry (Larson, 2004). Harriet's parents were slaves to different people. Rit was enslaved by Mary Pattison Brodess and later on by her son Edward as the Brodess family cook while Ben was the slave of Anthony Thompson, the second husband of Mary Brodess. Thompson ran a large plantation near to the Blackwater River in the Madison area of Dorchester County, New York, and Ben was a skilled woodsman who managed the timber work on the plantation. Ben and Rit married around 1808 and had nine children together: Linah, Mariah Ritty, Soph, Robert, Minty (Harriet), Ben, Rachel, Henry, and Moses.

Harriet does not seem to have had much of a childhood, as it seems her life was full of work and responsibilities from an early age. She had no formal education and was illiterate, but she was told Bible stories by her mother and likely attended a Methodist church with her family. As Harriet's mother worked in "the big house," Rit had little time for her own family, which meant that the older children had to take care of the younger ones. As a child, Harriet was responsible for the care of a younger brother and a baby before the age of five. Such responsibilities were typical in larger families in the early 19th century. Her working life began early, too. When Harriet was around five or six, Brodess hired her out as a nursemaid to a lady named "Miss Susan." She was responsible for taking care of a baby and rocking the cradle while it slept. If the baby woke up or cried, Harriet was whipped. She later recalled that on a particular day at Miss Susan's, she was lashed five times before breakfast and carried the scars from that punishment for the rest of her life. After six months of this brutal treatment, Harriet was returned to her parents, sick, battered, and unable to work.

This unjust punishment fostered a spirit of resistance in young Harriet. She began to fight back, wore layers of clothing to protect herself against beatings, and once even ran away for five days. Rodriguez (2007) remarks that Harriet's early experiences at Miss Susan's gave her protection skills that served her well in later life. For example, from this time onwards Harriet encouraged the idea that she was mentally impaired to avoid her slave master using her for breeding purposes. This caused him to believe her to be half-witted and it not to be worth the risk of her bearing his child.

Then aged six, Harriet was sent to work for a planter named James Cook. He lived 10 miles from her family home, and she was there to learn the weaver's trade. One of her jobs at Cook's was to wade out into the water to check the muskrat traps in nearby marshes. She even had to complete this task when she was ill with measles, leading Harriet to become so ill that Cook sent her back to Brodess, where her mother nursed her back to health. Once she had recovered, she was sent back to Cook, where she refused to learn weaving because she hated her mistress. Instead, by the time she was a teenager, Harriet was hired out as a farmhand and tasked with field and forest work, which included driving oxen, plowing, and handling logs.

Forced separations from home meant that Harriet was often homesick as a child. Later on in life, she would compare herself to "the boy on the Swanee River," an allusion to Stephen Foster's song "Old Folks at Home." Although she was unable to read and write, Harriet was extremely strong and had a great deal of ingenuity. For example, she convinced her owner to hire her out as a field hand on the condition she pay him $1 a day and any extra money she earned would belong to her. She worked so hard that she was able to buy two steers for $40 and, eventually, aimed to earn enough money through this strategy to gain her freedom. This anecdote from Harriet's childhood hints at the depth of her yearning for freedom from a young age and the lengths to which she would be prepared to go in later life to achieve her goals.

Significant Events

Two significant events took place in Harriet's childhood that seem to have influenced her later work in the abolitionist movement.

First, Harriet's mother, Rit, made an impassioned attempt to keep her family together despite the cruel conditions imposed by slavery. Edward Brodess sold three of her daughters (Linah, Mariah Ritty, and Soph) and this distressing event made Rit cling fiercely onto her other children and resist any attempt made to sell them. So, when a trader from Georgia approached Brodess about buying Rit's youngest son, Moses, she hid him for a month with the help of other slaves and freedmen in the local community. When Brodess and "the Georgia man" came to the slave quarters to seize Moses, Rit threatened to split the head open of the first man who came into her home, and Brodess backed down from the sale. This act of defiance seems to have shown Harriet that it was possible to resist slavery.

Second, perhaps one of the seminal events of Harriet's life, was the head injury she received when aged 13 and working as a field hand. An overseer attempting to whip a slave who had left his work and gone to a crossroads store threw a 2 lb weight at the runaway. However, it missed and struck Harriet "a stunning blow on the head" after she had, with others, attempted to intervene between overseer and slave (Sernett, 2007, p. 16). Later, Harriet recalled:

> The weight broke my skull… They carried me to the house all bleeding and fainting. I had no bed, no place to lie down on at all, and they laid me on the seat of the loom, and I stayed there all day and the next. (History.com Editors, 2023b, p. 1)

Despite the severity of her injuries, Harriet did not receive any medical care for two days. As a result of the head injury, Harriet frequently experienced painful headaches and would experience blackouts for the rest of her life. She also began having frequent seizures and often fell unconscious, suddenly appearing to be asleep. These episodes lasted from several minutes to over an hour. She claimed that she was aware of her surroundings, although she appeared to be asleep during episodes. Larson (2004) suggests that Harriet's head injury triggered temporal lobe epilepsy while Clinton (2004) proposes that she may have had cataplexy or narcolepsy. Whatever condition Harriet developed as a result of her head injuries, she had it for the rest of her life. However, lack of contemporary evidence makes a definitive diagnosis impossible.

A significant after-effect of Harriet's injury was that she began to experience visions and vivid dreams that she believed were revelations from God. These visions encouraged her to reject the teachings of White preachers who urged enslaved people to be passive and obedient victims of their enslavers and masters. Instead, she found guidance in Old Testament tales of deliverance. These religious experiences and her interpretation of them would influence Harriet's actions for the rest of her life. Later on, Harriet's religious visions would particularly impress her admirers, such as Sarah Hopkins Bradford (1818–1912), who wrote two books about Harriet. Bradford (1869) observed:

> When these turns of somnolence come upon Harriet, she imagines that her "spirit" leaves her body, and visits other scenes and places, not only in this world, but also in the world of spirits... Not long since, the writer, on going into Harriet's room in the morning, sat down by her and began to read that wonderful and glorious description of the heavenly Jerusalem in the two last chapters of Revelations. When the reading was finished, Harriet burst into a rhapsody which perfectly amazed the hearer—telling of what she had seen in one of these visions, sights which no one could doubt had been real to hear, and which no human imagination could have conceived, it would seem, unless in dream or vision. (pp. 55-56)

Her head injury thus seems to have changed Harriet's views on life, making it possible for her to follow the path that she did and gave her the belief that her actions were sanctioned by some divine power.

Early Adulthood and Escape

Harriet's early adult life was dominated by attempts by herself and other family members to escape the bonds of slavery. First, her father's master, Anthony Thompson, had promised to manumit him at the age of 45. After Thompson died, his son followed through with that promise in 1840. Despite gaining his freedom, Ben Ross continued to work as a foreman and timber estimator for the Thompson family. However, while Ben Ross was now free, his wife and children were not, as the status of the mother dictated that of the children. This was the legal doctrine of *partus sequitur ventrem*, passed in colonial Virginia in 1662.

Harriet's own marriage may have also been part of a strategy to free herself from slavery. Around 1844, she married a free Black man named John Tubman, who then came to live with her at the plantation's slave quarters. Not much is known about their time together, but it appears that the union might have been complicated by Harriet's enslaved status. However, marriages between enslaved and free Black people were common in the Eastern Shore of Maryland at that time, as around half of the Black population was free. Despite any complications that might have emerged as a result of her marriage, Larson (2004) suggests that Harriet's union with Tubman was part of a strategy to buy her freedom.

What is certain is that soon after her marriage, Harriet changed her name from Araminta to Harriet. It is unclear exactly when this happened. It has been suggested Minty began to be known as Harriet immediately after her wedding. Alternatively, the name change may have coincided with Harriet's eventual escape from slavery. Choosing her mother's name as her new name may have been part of Harriet's religious conversion or to honor another relative.

Harriet also made a conscious effort to free her mother. In the late 1840s, she paid a lawyer $5 ($160 in 2023) to investigate Rit's legal status. The lawyer discovered that Atthow Pattison, the grandfather of Mary Brodess, had indicated in his will that Rit and any of her children would be manumitted at the age of 45, and any children born after she reached the age of 45 would be freed. But the Pattison and Brodess families ignored this stipulation when they inherited Rit and her children. Despite the illegality of their master's actions, it was impossible for Harriet to raise the money to take the legal action required to enforce the will of Atthow Pattison. Eventually, on June 1, 1855, Ben purchased his wife's freedom for $20 from Eliza Ann Brodess at the local courthouse. At this point, Rit was around 70-years-old and had spent her entire lifetime as a slave.

In early 1849, Harriet heard a rumor that herself and two of her brothers were to be sold. At that time, she was also ill, which diminished her value for slave traders. Consequently, when Edward Brodess tried to sell her, he was unable to find a buyer. Nevertheless, Harriet also prayed to God to make sure that Bodress would not sell her. Ultimately though, it seemed that a sale might be concluded so, on March 1, 1849, she prayed, "Oh Lord, if you ain't never going to change that man's heart, kill him, Lord, and take him out of the way" (Walters, 2020, p. 44). The following week, Brodess died, and Harriet regretted her earlier prayer.

Brodess's death also meant that it was more likely that Harriet would be sold and separated from her family, as his widow, Eliza, who had inherited her late husband's slaves, decided to sell some of her new slaves. Reluctant to wait for her new mistress to decide her fate, Harriet, despite the misgivings of her husband, vowed to escape. Later, she recalled that it was a matter of "liberty or death; if I could not have one, I would have the other" (Walters, 2020, p. 47).

Harriet's religious visions gave her the strength to finally decide to escape. Having witnessed two of her sisters sold farther into the South, Harriet had a vision of a group of horsemen riding into the slave quarters at night. She heard the slaves cry out in agony as children were torn from their parents' arms. In another vision, Harriet saw her own escape, seeing the faces of all her liberators.

Later, Harriet would claim that the faces were those of members of the Underground Railroad who helped her achieve freedom. Many of her dreams of freedom were full of "green fields and lovely flowers, and beautiful white ladies, who stretched out their arms to me other than the line" (Rodriguez, 2007, p. 533). These visions alongside the rumor about the sale of her and her brothers ultimately gave Harriet the courage to leave.

On September 17, 1849, Harriet accompanied by two of her brothers, Ben and Henry, escaped for the first time. Harriet had been hired out to the son of her father's former owner, Anthony Thompson, Jr., to work at his large plantation, Poplar Neck, in Caroline County. This also appears to have been where her brothers were working. As they had been hired out, their mistress did not realize that the three siblings were missing for a fortnight, when she posted a runaway notice in the *Cambridge Democrat*. Here she offered a reward of up to $100 ($3,520 in 2023) for their capture and return to her. However, the escape attempt was short-lived as her brothers both had second thoughts, with Ben regretting leaving his wife and children behind. Thus, her brothers returned home, forcing Harriet to do so with them.

But Harriet soon had a chance to escape again. At some point in October or November 1849, she ran away once again without her brothers. She signaled her escape to a fellow slave, Mary, by singing a farewell song: "I'll meet you in the morning... I'm bound for the promised land"

(Larson, 2004, pp. 82–83). It is unknown exactly how she escaped, but she did make use of the Underground Railroad, an informal system made up of free and enslaved Black people, White abolitionists, and other anti-slavery activists, mostly consisting of the Quakers in Maryland. The substantial Quaker community in the Preston area near Poplar Neck most likely provided initial assistance during Harriet's escape. From there, Harriet undertook a journey of 90 miles on foot, spanning between five days and three weeks. To avoid slave catchers, Harriet had to travel at night, guided by the North Star. During the day, she would appear to be working for the families that hid her, or she would hide in the woods and marshes that she was so familiar with. Then, at night, she would be transported to the next friendly house. Some of her hosts are known to us. She first traveled toward Camden, Delaware, to the home of Eliza and Ezekiel Hamm and from Camden she was assisted by the noted Quaker abolitionist, Thomas Garrett.

She felt profound relief when she finally reached Philadelphia and safety, later recalling that "I felt like I was in heaven" (Walters, 2020, p. 52). Eventually, Harriet settled in Philadelphia, where she found friends and shelter and became better acquainted with the secretive Underground Railroad.

The Underground Railroad

Harriet was now free thanks to the Underground Railroad, a network of safe houses and secret routes created during the early- to mid-19th century to help enslaved African Americans to escape to the free states and, from there, to Canada. Once Harriet had successfully escaped and set herself up in Philadelphia, her thoughts turned to her family, many of whom were still enslaved. Having managed to escape using the assistance and resources offered by the Underground Railroad, she decided to become part of that network to help her family and others escape slavery. She realized that she would not truly be free as long as members of her family were still slaves. Harriet later explained: "I was free but there was no one to welcome me to the land of freedom" (Rodriguez, 2007, p. 533). So, Harriet became involved in the Underground Railroad to make sure that her family, like herself, could experience the liberating feeling of being free. In Philadelphia, Harriet worked as a laundress, cook, scrub woman, and seamstress to earn enough money to finance her trips to the South for the Underground Railroad.

Her first trip as a conductor on the Underground Railroad was made to free one of her sisters (in fact, her niece, Kessiah) and her sister's two children. Kessiah is often referred to as Harriet's sister as this is how Harriet and Kessiah saw one another. In December 1850, Harriet got word that Kessiah and her children were to be sold in Cambridge. Upon hearing the news, she immediately traveled to Baltimore, where she was hidden by her brother-in-law, Tom Tubman, until the sale. Kessiah's husband, John Bowley, who was a free Black man, made the winning bid on his wife. As the auctioneer took a break to have lunch, John, Kessiah, and their children escaped to a safe house nearby. At nightfall, Bowley then sailed his family in a long canoe for 60 miles to Baltimore, where they met with Harriet, who brought the family to Philadelphia.

On her next trip, she freed her brother and two others. Then in 1851, Harriet returned again to guide her husband, John, to safety but instead found him living with another woman and uninterested in freedom. Instead, she led 11 slaves to freedom, including another brother and his family.

In total, Harriet made 19 trips into Maryland, Delaware, and Virginia, freeing over 300 people. It was dangerous work and usually took place during winter when the long nights and cold weather decreased the chances of being seen. Harriet tended to start escapes on Saturday evenings as the newspapers would not print notices until Monday morning, allowing more time for an escape. She was never once captured and never lost a passenger, making her the most effective conductor to ever work the Underground Railroad. As a result of her success as a conductor, her admirers called her "Moses," after the Biblical Moses who led the Jews from Egypt. The slaves who she helped to escape swore she had supernatural abilities that helped her conduct them to safety, saying that she had the eyesight of an eagle, the hearing of a deer, and the ability to quell dogs at a glance. The great abolitionist and orator Frederick Douglass would later write to Harriet, praising her:

> Most that I have done and suffered in the service of our cause has been in public, and I have received much encouragement at every step of the way. You, on the other hand, have labored in a private way. I have wrought in the day—you in the night. (Library of Congress, 1998, p. 1)

Because of Harriet's effectiveness as a conductor, slave owners lost tens of millions of dollars in property due to her actions, leading Southern legislators to call for her capture, dead or alive. Legend has it that at one point there was a $40,000 reward offered for her recapture. This story appears to have originated in Bradford's second edition of her biography of Harriet, *Harriet, the Moses of Her People*, published in 1886. Instead, it has been proposed that a figure of $1,200 or $12,000 is more plausible, as Harriet was indeed a "significant catch for Southern bounty hunters" (Sernett, 2007, p. 67).

Despite the price placed on her head, Harriet continued to come to the aid of fleeing slaves. Another potential danger for conductors arose in 1850, when the defenders of slavery persuaded Congress to pass the Fugitive Slave Law, which required all escaped slaves to be returned to their masters without question or a trial. This is because the new law empowered slave owners to legally claim that a slave had escaped. That claim would then serve as proof of a person's slave status, even in free states and territories. Specially appointed feudal commissioners adjudicated the identity of alleged fugitives, and the commissioners were paid fees that favored slaveholders: $10 if the alleged fugitive was returned, and $5 if not.

The Underground Railroad responded by increasing its efforts to help slaves flee to Canada. As a consequence of this new law, Harriet also had to go back on the road to avoid capture. From Philadelphia, she was sent to Rochester, New York by the Black abolitionist, William Still. In Rochester, she met the abolitionist and women's rights advocate Susan B. Anthony, who then encouraged her to go to Lake Erie. After crossing Lake Erie, Harriet entered Saint Catherine's, Canada, where she lived between 1851 and 1857.

From Canada, Harriet made two trips a year to the South, eventually succeeding in freeing her entire family, including her parents. Between 1851 and 1862, Harriet returned to the Eastern Shore of Maryland several times, undertaking 13 expeditions and rescuing around 70 slaves. The escapees included her brothers Robert, Ben, and Henry, their wives, and some of their children. During this period, Harriet also gave specific guidance to around 50 to 60 other enslaved people who successfully escaped.

In one of her final journeys to Maryland, Harriet collected her aging parents. Although her father had purchased her mother in 1855, the area they lived in was hostile. In 1857, Harriet heard that her father could be arrested because he had sheltered eight people escaping slavery. So, she collected her parents and took them north to Saint Catherine's to join the community of formerly enslaved people there, many of whom were relatives and friends of the family.

Espionage

During the American Civil War, Harriet acted as a scout for Union military operations. Between 1862 and 1864, she worked for the Department of the South, located on a group of islands off the coast of South Carolina where Reconstruction was already taking place. When President Abraham Lincoln issued the Emancipation Proclamation on January 1, 1863, Harriet saw it as a positive step but felt that the movement to liberate all slaves remained incomplete. Instead, she decided she needed to take more direct action to defeat the Confederacy. To this end, Harriet utilized her knowledge of hiding and covert travel to lead a group of scouts through the land around Port Royal. The group worked under the orders of the Secretary of War, Edwin Stanton, to map the terrain. She then worked with Colonel James Montgomery and gave him key intelligence that allowed the Union Army to capture Jacksonville, Florida.

Later in 1863, Harriet's intelligence-gathering efforts played a seminal role in the raid at Combahee Ferry. Under Montgomery's command, she guided three steamboats with Black soldiers past mines placed in the Combahee River, allowing them to assault several plantations. The Union troops then set fire to the plantations, an act that destroyed key Confederacy infrastructure, and they also seized food and supplies worth thousands of dollars. During the raid, many enslaved people in the area were freed. Liberation was signaled by the sound of the steamboats' whistles, which prompted the slaves to stampede toward the boats. Harriet later recalled a chaotic scene with pigs squealing in bags thrown over shoulders, women carrying pots of rice that were still steaming, and babies hanging around the necks of their parents (Clinton, 2004). Although armed overseers tried to stop the escape, their efforts were futile. Confederate troops then appeared on the scene but, by then, the steamboats were headed toward Beaufort, taking over 750 formerly enslaved people with them.

Harriet's service to the Union Army was informal in nature, although she was later praised for rendering "invaluable service in the Union Army as a spy, scout, and hospital nurse" (Sernett, 2007, p. 87). She did so as a volunteer without formal training but is nevertheless considered to be a Black nursing pioneer today. In addition to serving as a secret agent and scout, Harriet also served as a liaison between the Union Army and local slaves.

Later Years

Harriet stayed in the Union Army until 1865. She then returned to her home in Auburn, New York to care for her elderly parents. During that time, she met a veteran named Nelson Davis. The two married in 1869 and adopted a daughter, Gertie in 1874. After the war, Harriet focused her energies on women's rights and helping the poor, undertaking many of her works through the National Association of Colored Women. Because of her religious convictions, Harriet also worked closely with Black charities, soliciting donations of used clothing and food for the poor and elderly in New York State. She also helped to set up schools for freed slaves.

While Harriet is commonly portrayed as a leader in the women's suffrage movement, her role in such activities appears to have been exaggerated. She did agree with the proposition that women should have the vote, but she never actively assisted the suffragists or the women's suffrage movement, although she did many other good works.

Because she was so generous to others, Harriet was often penniless herself. Petitions to the War Department on her behalf for a pension for services rendered by her were unsuccessful; however, in 1890, she finally secured a widow's pension for the services rendered by her second husband, Nelson Davis, in the Union Army. During tough times, Harriet supplemented her income by selling photographs of herself, justifying this by stating that selling her image kept the substance alive.

Harriet's final philanthropic action was to start a care home for elderly Black people, which eventually opened in 1908. In 1896, she used money from her own meager store to buy a small parcel of land adjacent to her home to build a home for the elderly poor, which came to be operated by the African Methodist Episcopal Zion Church. She became an invalid in her old age and lived the last two years of her life at the Harriet Tubman Home for the Aged and Indigent Colored People until her death. Harriet died of pneumonia on March 10, 1913, surrounded by family members and friends and was buried at Fort Hill Cemetery in Auburn, New York with semi-military honors.

Perhaps fittingly, Harriet's last words were a direct quote from the Gospel of St John as she told her friends and family, "I go away to prepare a place for you," much as she had done when she helped them escape slavery all those years ago (Dunbar, 2019, p. 133).

Harriet's Cultural Legacy

Harriet's cultural legacy has flourished in the years following her death. She has been honored with a United States postage stamp, and her home in Auburn, New York is recognized as a national landmark. Also, during the Second World War, a liberty ship was christened SS *Harriet Tubman*. Most recently, it has been announced that a Harriet Tubman $20 bill will be released in 2030.

In recent years, a museum and a film have been created to honor Harriet's legacy. The Harriet Tubman Underground Railroad Visitor Center, located in Church Creek on Maryland's Eastern Shore, opened to the public in March 2017. The location of the museum reflects the fact that it is located in the region Harriet escaped slavery from and would go on to return to over 13 times between 1850 and 1862 to free around 70 family members and friends.

The 2019 film *Harriet* stars Cynthia Erivo as Harriet and begins with her 1849 escape. The narrative then chronicles her trips to the South to free her family from slavery. The plot focuses on liberation and solidarity rather than the pain, trauma, and humiliation of slavery. Praise for *Harriet* states that: "So often, historical films are stale and mired in misery, but *Harriet* has a rare buoyancy" (Hans, 2019, p. 1). A similar statement could be made about Harriet's own life. Her existence in slavery could have been stale and miserable, but Harriet herself had a rare buoyancy that allowed her to seek freedom and lead many others to the same.

Chapter Two
The Grimké Sisters
Trailblazers of Activism

This chapter focuses on Sarah and Angelina Grimké, two sisters from South Carolina who became abolitionists and women's rights activists. Here we explore their upbringing, their conversion to Quakerism, and their advocacy for the abolition of slavery and women's suffrage. Unlike Harriet Tubman, the sisters came from a privileged background and were well-educated. Sarah and Angelina published pamphlets and went on lecture circuits. Coming from a slave-owning family, the sisters were slowly awakened to the horrors of slavery and found like-minded people in the abolitionist movement and the Quaker movement, although the latter disapproved of their controversial lectures. They were also good friends with Elizabeth Cady Stanton. All this and more is discussed below.

Upbringing and Awakening

Sarah Moore Grimké was born on November 26, 1792, and Angelina Emily Grimké on February 20, 1805, both in Charleston, South Carolina. Sarah and Angelina were part of a large family, being the sixth and youngest respectively in a family totaling 14 children. They were the daughters of John Faucheraud Grimké (1752–1819) and Mary Smith. Their mother came from a wealthy and influential Charleston family while their father was an American jurist and wealthy planter of Huguenot descent who held thousands of slaves. He owned a fashionable townhouse in Charleston and many other properties in the local area, including a large plantation on the coast near Beaufort, South Carolina.

The sisters were educated by tutors, mainly in the ornamental arts, as were many women of similar social status at that time. Their education was that of the well-bred Southern girl, which included learning a little French, watercolor techniques, harpsichord techniques, and white-on-white embroidery. Sarah's most bitter disappointment was being denied an education as she had remarkable intellectual gifts that were evident from an early age. However, in that time and place, such talents were unwelcome in a girl. She later reflected: "Man has done all he could to debase and enslave [woman's] mind" (Nies, 1977, p. 11). Sarah had loved learning and initially studied with an older brother and had ambitions to go to college. Her goal in this was to eventually practice law like her brother. Even at the age of 12, she studied legal codes at night and plotted to go to college. However, her father forbade her from continuing her studies, instead insisting she pursue the course of womanly studies outlined above.

Despite this, her father did permit her to teach herself using the books in his library even whilst denying her the education that was provided to her brothers.

Having witnessed the cruelty of slavery from earliest childhood, both Sarah and Angelina grew up to despise the practice. Their father held his children up to the highest standards of discipline and sometimes required them to spend time working in the plantation fields, shelling corn or picking cotton. Sarah later acknowledged: "Perhaps I am indebted partially to this for my lifelong detestation of slavery, as it brought me in close contact with the unpaid toilers" (National Park Service, 2015, p. 1).

During their childhoods, both sisters were awakened to the horrors of slavery. According to Sarah: "slavery… marred my comfort from the time I can remember myself" (Nies, 1977, p. 9). When she was five-years-old, she accidentally witnessed the whipping of a domestic servant. Sarah was so upset by what she had witnessed she fled to a local wharf and asked a sea captain to take her to some place where such things were not done. This childhood perception that under slavery one could only either be a victim or victimizer remained with her all her life. Meanwhile, Angelina was particularly horrified by the violence of the institution of slavery, having heard painful cries from men, women, and even children being whipped and having seen the lingering scars on the bodies of the slaves that served her on a daily basis. The sisters also heard stories of the dreaded Charleston Workhouse that, for a fee, would administer beatings and various other forms of torture out of sight of slave-owning households. These formative experiences would inspire their later abolitionist activities.

Defying Social Norms

In childhood, both sisters displayed rebellious behaviors and attitudes that challenged the status quo of the early 19th-century American South. Sarah and Angelina taught some slaves to read and write and held prayer meetings with others, although their parents told them not to do so. Aged eight, Sarah began teaching in the slave children's Sunday school. Black children were not supposed to learn to read and write so were to only receive oral instruction. Instead of obeying this regulation, Sarah tried to let the children look at her catechism to learn the same way she had, but the older teachers sternly reprimanded her for doing so. In another instance, when their father discovered that Sarah had taught her servant and contemporary, Kitty, to read, he warned her about the criminal nature of her activity, telling her that it went against the law of South Carolina, which forbade teaching slaves to read and write and that she could be punished with a large fine or even imprisonment. Angelina also tried to make the family abandon slavery, but to no avail. Sarah described taking "malicious satisfaction" in defying both her parents and South Carolina law by teaching her "little waiting maid" and a number of other slaves to read and write (Faust, 2022, p. 1).

Sarah was 13-years-old when Angelina was born and insisted on becoming her godmother. Already alarmed by Sarah's "unwomanly" aspirations, her parents tried to talk her out of her plan but ultimately agreed to it, deciding that being Angelina's godmother was potentially less dangerous than her desire to become a woman lawyer. As Angelina's godmother, Sarah promised "to guide and direct [this] precious child" (National Park Service, 2015, p. 1). For the next 30 years, Angelina would refer to Sarah as "mother" and, in turn, Sarah took responsibility for Angelina's development, inventing new games and challenging her with new ideas. Through her close involvement with Angelina's upbringing, Sarah helped to create a secure, independent, imaginative, emotionally stable young woman who would also play a critical role in the anti-slavery movement. Sarah's commitment as Angelina's godmother foreshadowed the lifelong bond the sisters shared with one another and strengthened Sarah's determination to fight for social justice.

As a young woman, Sarah threw herself into the parties and social life of Charleston and various religious enthusiasms, but soon realized that she was unsuited to being a wife and mother, although she had no alternative apart from continuing to live with her family. However, all this changed when John Grimké became ill in 1819 and had to go to Philadelphia for medical treatment and insisted

26-year-old Sarah accompany him. There, John Grimké died, and Sarah became free to chart her own course in life. Also, during her stay in Philadelphia, Sarah met members of the Society of Friends, otherwise known as the Quakers, who helped her care for her dying father. This encounter would shape the rest of the sisters' lives. First, though, immediately after her father's death, Sarah returned to Charleston, where her opposition to slavery soon reasserted itself. She later recalled:

> After being for many months in Pennsylvania when I went back it seemed as if the sight of [the slaves'] condition was insupportable... can compare my feeling only with a canker incessantly gnawing... I was as one in bonds looking on the sufferings I could not soothe or lessen. (National Park Service, 2015, p. 1)

Aged 28, Sarah decided to leave South Carolina and move to Philadelphia. Her decision was due to her conversion to Quakerism, which made it impossible to remain in Charleston as her conversion had made her a social outcast. Angelina, who also had developed a horror of slavery, also converted to Quakerism in 1829 and moved to Philadelphia to join her sister.

Soon, however, the sisters were also at odds with their new Quaker friends in Philadelphia. In 1835, Angelina wrote a personal letter to the abolitionist William Lloyd Garrison that was published by him in the anti-slavery newspaper *The Liberator*. In her letter, Angelina encouraged Garrison to stand up for what he believed in, even when confronted with violence:

> If persecution is the means which God has ordained for the accomplishment of this great end, emancipation, then... I feel as if I could say, let it come; for it is my deep, solemn deliberate conviction, that this is a cause worth dying for. (National Park Service, 2015, p. 1)

The letter caused outrage among the sisters' Quaker friends, who believed that it was a sign that Angelina was a radical abolitionist. Angelina was put under considerable pressure to recall it; however, she chose not to do so, although standing her ground made her and her sister social outcasts in Quaker circles. Instead, in the summer of 1835, Angelina publicly joined the abolitionist movement, thereby ending her ties with the Quaker community.

In the summer of 1836, Elizur Wright offered Angelina a position as an abolitionist agent. However, Angelina was not quite ready to commit herself to the anti-slavery cause in that way. Feeling that she had to do something, Angelina wrote an appeal to the fellow Christian women she

THE GRIMKÉ SISTERS   29

had left in the South when she emigrated north. Over the course of her two-week summer vacation in New Jersey, Angelina wrote her *Appeal to the Christian Women of the South*, which was subsequently printed and widely distributed by the American Anti-Slavery Society. This essay marked the sisters' complete immersion in the abolitionist movement as, within a few months, Angelina, Sarah, and 40 other abolitionists undertook four weeks of abolitionist-agent training under Angelina's future husband, Theodore Weld. In 1837, the sisters became the first female agents of the American Anti-Slavery Society.

These steps made the sisters influential members of the abolitionist movement, something further bolstered by their powerful speeches and writings that gave a voice to the voiceless. The sisters began their careers as public speakers in the fall of 1836 when they were invited to speak publicly to a group in New York City. This step marked a new stage in Sarah and Angelina's careers as activists, and they traveled all over the Northeast, giving talks on abolition and women's rights. The women's contributions in this area were sought out and valued because of their experiences growing up in a slave-holding family. This meant that they intimately understood the system of slavery in a way most Northern abolitionists did not. Their public speaking activities were incredibly popular with their fellow abolitionists. For example, during their 1837 tour, they lectured to 1,500 people in Lowell, Massachusetts, and their three lectures in Salem attracted 2,400 listeners

(Durso, 2003). The women toured New York and New Jersey writing and lecturing on the evils of slavery, despite being criticized by church ministers for their unwomanly behavior. Sarah and Angelina's speeches focused on arguing for the equality of the Black population and drew heavily on scripture, evoking Biblical insight in their quest for justice.

Angelina in particular was a powerful speaker and considered to be one of the best in the abolitionist movement. In 1838, she became the first American woman to address a legislative body when she spoke to the Massachusetts State Legislature about abolition and women's rights. On that occasion, she presented a petition signed by 20,000 women, all of whom sought the end of slavery.

Challenging the Status Quo

The purpose of the sisters' involvement in the abolition and women's rights movements was to challenge the status quo around such matters. Angelina explained the purpose of the sister's activities in the following way:

> I am trying to talk down, and write down, and live down this horrible prejudice... we must dig up this weed by the roots out of each of our hearts. (Murrill, 2021, p. 1)

Initially, they embarked on their anti-slavery activities despite the disapproval of the Quaker community to which they belonged when Angelina published her article in *The Liberator* in 1835, launching the sisters' careers as abolitionist writers and speakers. Then, in her *Appeal to the Christian Women of the South* (1836), Angelina encouraged white Southern women to join the abolitionist movement. She wrote:

> I know you do not make the laws, but I also know that you are the wives and mothers, the sisters and daughters of those who do; and if you really suppose you can do nothing to overthrow slavery, you are greatly mistaken. (National Park Service, 2015, p. 1)

This tract was widely criticized by both Southerners and Northerners, as the former opposed its abolitionist message and the latter felt that women should not speak or write about something as controversial as slavery. Around the same time, Sarah released her own abolitionist work, *Epistle to the Clergy of the Southern States*. This work also incited the outrage of leaders in the South, who burnt both Sarah and Angelina's books and warned their mother that if her daughters returned to Charleston, they would be arrested. At one point, a raid of the Charleston Post Office took place, and incoming writings by the sisters were burnt. These actions demonstrate the strong opposition to the sisters' abolitionism and their decision to speak out as women. Indeed, the outcry over the idea that women could be abolitionists prompted Sarah to write and publish her *Letters on the Equality of the Sexes* (1837).

By the late 1830s, the sisters were not just famous for being abolitionists but also as promoters of women's rights. The resistance to their speaking and writing due to their status as women encouraged Sarah and Angelina to speak about the equality of women as well as the abolition of slavery. However, their strong stance on both issues made them outcasts in both the abolitionist and women's rights movements. This is because many abolitionists did not believe that women should speak or write publicly, while many campaigners for women's rights did not endorse the abolition of slavery.

Nevertheless, in the 1840s, the sisters' contributions to the women's rights movements were more widely recognized. Although Sarah and Angelina did not attend the first women's rights convention held at Seneca Falls, New York in 1848, Sarah was invited to the event by Elizabeth Cady Stanton, as proven by a letter by the former to Elizabeth M'Clintock. In July 1848, Stanton wrote to M'Clintock that "I have written to... Sarah Grimké, as we hope for some good letters to read at the convention." The Stantons and Grimkés were good friends. Elizabeth's husband, Henry, was best man at the wedding of Angelina and Theodore Weld, and the Stantons' eldest sons attended the boarding school run by Theodore and the sisters. Also,

Elizabeth and Henry named their fourth son Theodore Weld Stanton after Angelina's husband.

While Sarah remained conservative in her thinking on moral questions and never could come to favor divorce, she did support women's suffrage. She said:

> Since the legislative body is the medium of communication between the government and various classes of society, it would seem but justice that women, who form one half of every class, should be participating in it. (Lerner, 1998, p. 249)

Sarah felt that granting the vote to women would be a great blessing for society, as would granting the franchise to foreign-born immigrants. Both sisters manifested their continuing interest in the cause of women by subscribing to the early feminist papers, such as *The Una*, edited by Paulina W. Davis, and *The Lily*, edited by Amelia Bloomer. The latter was a temperance paper with a strongly feminist editorial bias.

In 1852, the sisters adopted the Bloomer costume, consisting of a tunic, a short skirt, and pantaloons fastened at the ankles. This form of dress was designed to liberate women from the uncomfortable and unhealthy garments demanded by fashion (Lerner, 1998). The Bloomer costume appealed to reformers, whose philosophy inclined them towards simplicity in dress and diet and was a symbol of revolt against all the senseless restrictions imposed on women, as Sarah and Angelina had firsthand experience of. When Henry David Thoreau visited the sisters at Eagleswood, New Jersey in 1856, he wrote: "There sat Mrs. Weld and her sister, two elderly gray-haired ladies, the former in extreme Bloomer costume, which was what you might call remarkable" (Fladeland, 1971, p. 99). Both sisters wore the garment for a time, as did their friend Elizabeth Stanton.

Silencing the Sisters

As we have seen, the activities of the Grimké sisters in the 1830s were not welcomed by everyone. Many abolitionists thought that it was inappropriate for women to speak and write publicly about the subject, many women's rights campaigners did not support anti-slavery campaigning, and the sisters were no longer welcome in their home state of South Carolina. As their fame increased, the backlash also only increased. It was widely felt that Sarah and Angelina had behaved in a way contrary to what was expected of "respectable women." Many individuals were outraged that Sarah and Angelina spoke in front of audiences that contained both men and women as well as Black and White people mingling together. For example, a group of ministers complained that the behavior of attendees at their speeches violated God's order and was "unnatural" (Women and the American Story, 2023a). However, Sarah and Angelina disagreed and believed that they were doing God's work, so they continued to defend the right of women to speak against slavery in public and did not give into such widespread condemnation.

Things came to a head on Monday, May 14, 1838, when a four-day abolitionist convention opened in Philadelphia. It was the first event to take place in Pennsylvania Hall, which had been built by abolitionists as a meeting space, as the unpopularity of abolitionism made it difficult to find spaces to meet in. That same night, Angelina married Theodore Dwight Weld, one of America's leading abolitionists, with both Black and White abolitionists in attendance at the ceremony. Angelina spoke at the annual anti-slavery convention in Philadelphia two days after her marriage. That same evening, an anti-abolitionist mob, made up of angry Northern whites who were outraged by the presence of Black abolitionists at the meeting, gathered outside Pennsylvania Hall. Angelina's speech was disrupted several times by the mob, who threw rocks through the window when they saw Black and White women leaving the building arm in arm. The following day, the convention was canceled by the Mayor of Philadelphia in an effort to restore peace. However, the mob broke into the empty building and set it on fire. Firefighters made no effort to stop the blaze and, just days after it was built, the Pennsylvania Hall burnt to the ground.

Despite the popularity of their public speeches, the sisters' public abolitionist activities attracted a great deal of criticism. In 1836, leaders in the South had reacted to the sisters' public opposition to slavery by threatening to arrest them if they returned to the South. Also, the presence of men at speeches made by women was considered to be controversial, and Sarah and Angelina's activities were widely criticized by the clergy, male abolitionists, and even other women. The first public criticism of the Grimké sisters' abolitionist work came in early February 1837 when the New Haven *Religious Intelligencer* published a letter from a man only identified as "Clarkson." The letter argued that Northerners did not need Sarah and Angelina to "undeceive" them about the "wickedness, cruelty, and oppression of slavery" because they had been aware of the injustices of slavery for the past 40–50 years (Durso, 2003, p. 104). Thomas Clarkson also challenged the sisters to present "definitive practicable means" by which Northerners could put an end to slavery in the South (2003, p. 104).

The most damning criticism of Sarah and Angelina was made by the clergy of Massachusetts. Most famously, the Congregational Ministers' Association of Massachusetts made a public statement that condemned the sisters for speaking out while female. Also, in mid-1837, ministers belonging to the General Association of Massachusetts authorized the Reverend Nehemiah Adams of Boston to write a response to the abolition movement and the presence of female leaders in that movement. His work "Pastoral Letter of the Government Association of Massachusetts and the Congregational Churches Under Their Care" was read from pulpits and published in the July 12 edition of the *New England Spectator*. Adams's letter directly questioned whether abolitionism was a proper sphere of activity for women. Although his letter did not specifically mention the Grimké sisters, Adams clearly had them in mind when he denounced women who assumed "the place and tone of men as a public reformer" (Durso, 2003, p. 105). He also stated that "the appropriate duties and influence of women are clearly stated in the New Testament. These duties and that influence are unobtrusive and private" (2003, p. 105). Clearly, then, the clergy of Massachusetts believed that women should not express their views on abolitionism in public.

The views of Sarah and Angelina were even criticized by their female contemporaries, such as the prominent female educator Catharine Beecher, as she and her father, the Congregational minister Lyman Beecher, supported sending African Americans to Africa as a solution to slavery rather than outright abolition. Although Beecher had been friends with Sarah and Angelina since the 1820s, she published a pamphlet criticizing the abolition movement as being seriously misguided. This example shows how there were many discordant views regarding slavery in the circles the sisters were involved with.

As well as making public criticisms of Sarah and Angelina's activities, male leaders used a variety of insidious means to attempt to silence the sisters, such as ridiculing them and attempting to publicly portray them as unfeminine and ugly. The hostility toward the sisters and their views in some quarters can be demonstrated by the most famous images of the sisters. These are two wood engravings based on daguerreotypes taken of Sarah and Angelina in the 1840s, and which are now held by the Library of Congress as reproductions from a book in their collections. The original creator of the wood engravings has been lost to history. Indeed, even the date of creation is uncertain. While the existence of the daguerreotypes indicates that the images date to the 1840s, historian Louise W. Knight (2023) suggests the wood carvings first appeared in a periodical in the 1830s.

There are notable disparities between the original daguerreotypes and the wood engravings. In both images, Angelina is dressed the same, but the daguerreotype shows her with softer features, with a rounder face, lighter eyebrows, and more curved lips than the woman who appears in the wood engraving. On this basis, Knight (2023) theorizes that the wood carvings were satiric images, produced by someone who wanted to discredit the sisters' stance on abolition and women's rights by portraying them in a harsh manner. Such tactics were often used to discredit ideological and political opponents and were here used to imply that the sisters were not conventionally attractive enough to be desirable to men, and this was why they had taken to promoting such controversial ideas.

A similar trope is often used to discredit contemporary feminist scholars in the comments sections of online platforms today. Thus, these images can be interpreted as political cartoons rather than legitimate representations of Sarah and Angelina. The way in which the wood engravings were created to mock Sarah and Angelina is comparable to the misogyny prevalent today on social media, such as trolling and cancel culture.

Unfortunately, the hostility toward the sisters effectively silenced them, although some of their contemporaries such as Garrison and his New England friends believed that Angelina had been discouraged from voicing such a strong stance on abolitionism by her more moderate husband. Following their encounter with an anti-abolitionist mob in May 1838, Sarah and Angelina moved to New Jersey with Angelina's new husband, Theodore. The three would continue to live together for the rest of their lives. Angelina and Theodore had three children together: Charles Stuart (1839), Theodore Grimké (1841), and Sarah Grimké Weld (1844).

However, despite Sarah's aging and Angelina's commitments of marriage and motherhood, both sisters continued to write and support the abolitionist cause, although they ceased to have such a prominent role in the movement. Although they had retired from public speaking, the sisters continued to attend anti-slavery meetings and write abolitionist tracts, including *American Slavery as It Is* (1839), which was co-written by the sisters and Weld.

In later life, alongside Angelina's husband, Theodore,

the sisters ran schools in Belleville and Perth Amboy, New Jersey before moving to Massachusetts in 1863. They first settled in West Newton and, then in 1864, in the community of Hyde Park, south of Boston. There, Sarah, Angelina, and Theodore all taught at Dr. Dio Lewis's progressive School for Young Ladies in Lexington until its destruction by fire in 1867, and Sarah did some writing and translating.

In one of their final acts of compassion and sympathy toward the enslaved, after they learnt in 1868 that their brother Henry had fathered three children with an enslaved woman, they welcomed the children into their family and paid for their education. That year, Angelina came across a notice in an issue of the *National Anti-Slavery Standard* that referred to a meeting at Lincoln University where a Black student named Grimké had delivered an admirable address. Angelina wrote to the man, asking him if he had been the slave of one of her brothers. She was not surprised to receive a reply from Archibald that he was, in fact, her brother's son. He also told his aunt details about his early life and about his brothers Francis (Frank) and John. Angelina found his response "deeply... touching.: She was unable to change the past and her and Sarah's lack of knowledge about their nephews, but instead sought to establish a relationship with them in the present, expressing hope that they might redeem the family honor. "Grimké," she wrote to Archibald:

> Was one of the noblest names of Carolina... You, my young friend, now bear this once honored name—I charge you most solemnly by your upright conduct, and your life-long devotion to the eternal principles of justice and humanity and religion to lift this name out of the dust, where it now lies, and set it once more among the princes of our land. (Faust, 2022, p. 1)

This letter represented the beginnings of a relationship where the Welds provided financial assistance to Archibald at Harvard Law School and Frank at Princeton Theological College, encouraging the brothers to prove their excellence and worth as members of the Grimké family. However, the sisters viewed John as less talented and deserving than his brothers, leading him to become estranged from his family. Archibald and Frank also felt that their aunts put them under too much pressure to be successful.

Nevertheless, Archibald and Frank repaid their kindness by following in their footsteps and becoming civil rights activists themselves. Archibald was founder and vice president of the National Association for the Advancement of Colored People (NAACP) and later the American Consul for Santo Domingo, while Frank became a prominent member of the clergy and the Black elite of Washington, DC. The close ties between these two nephews and the Welds are further demonstrated by the fact that Frank decided to name his only child Theodora, and Archibald named his only daughter Angelina.

Throughout their lives, both Sarah and Angelina were advocates for women and people of color, although they were no longer active feminists in their later years. They did live to see one of their convictions proven when the Emancipation Proclamation was proclaimed in 1863 but would never see women get the vote.

However, the fact that the vote was never extended to women in Sarah and Angelina's lifetime did not stop them campaigning in this area until the very end of their lives. Another example of the sisters' radical nature continuing into their final years was their attempt to vote in a local election in 1870. Both sisters held the position of vice president of the Massachusetts Women's Suffrage Movement, founded in 1870. On March 7, 1870, they led a group of 42 women and a handful of male supporters to the Hyde Park Town Hall where they proceeded to cast illegal votes. The electoral official was an admirer of the Grimké sisters so allowed them and their friends to vote and place their ballots in a separate box. This meant that their votes were not counted as part of the official tally, but it did allow them to make their point. Although their votes were discounted, they are now on display at the Hyde Park Historical Society where they stand as an example of the efforts women made to secure the vote. At the time, their small action gained them and the suffrage cause considerable publicity. Throughout the 1870s, a number of copycat actions were undertaken by other suffragettes in the United States, albeit with less success than the original protest devised by the Grimké sisters.

Sarah died on December 23, 1873, aged 81, of laryngitis. Shortly afterwards, Angelina suffered a paralytic stroke that left her partially incapacitated. She died six years later on October 26, 1879, aged 74. Both sisters died at Hyde Park and were buried at Mount Hope Cemetery in Boston. Theodore Weld survived his wife of 15 years, and when he died, he was buried with Sarah and Angelina.

The Sisters' Cultural Legacy

In recent years, considerable efforts have been made by the Hyde Park Historical Society, based in the area where the sisters spent their final years, to honor Sarah and Angelina and acknowledge the role they played in American history. To this end, a new bridge over the Neponset River was named after them in 2019. Also, in the fall of 2021, a new marker was placed for Angelina in Mount Hope Cemetery, as her name was never carved on the original headstone, only Theodore and Sarah's. The gravestone that marks the grave of both sisters and Angelina's husband was also cleaned. These actions show that, although the sisters are no longer household names, people still appreciate what they did and acknowledge how extraordinary they were.

The sisters are also memorialized in fiction. One example is the January 2014 novel *The Invention of Wings* by Sue Monk Kidd. This novel chronicles the struggle and everyday rebellions of Sarah Grimké between 1803 and 1838 and also explores her relationship with a fictitious slave named Handful, who she is given as a gift for her 11th birthday. The focus of the novel is finding a voice to articulate pain when silenced, whether for being a woman, for being a slave, or both. *The Invention of Wings* brings the lives of the Grimké sisters to light and has also inspired a walking tour through downtown Charleston. The tour is available throughout the year and consists of a 2-hour and 15-minute walk that stops to highlight locations and events from the book. It tells untold stories about the sisters to give fans a better picture of the sisters and their lives.

These examples prove that people have not forgotten about the Grimké sisters and their achievements. Indeed, in recent years, there has been renewed commitment to reviving and honoring memories of the sisters and the integral role they played in abolitionist and feminist history.

Chapter Three
Sojourner Truth
The Unwavering Truth Seeker

This chapter will explore the life of Sojourner Truth, an escaped enslaved woman who became a prominent abolitionist and women's rights advocate. Here, we discuss her childhood, her escape from slavery, her work as a speaker and traveling preacher, and her activism, including her famous "Ain't I a Woman?" speech. We also touch on her involvement in the suffrage movement.

Early Life and Escape from Slavery

Sojourner Truth was born Isabella (Belle) Baumfree (or Bonefree), according to her own account, between 1797 and 1800 in Hurley, New York as one of ten to twelve children of slaves James and Elizabeth Baumfree. Her parents were slaves of Colonel Charles Hardenbergh and lived on his estate of Swartekill in the town of Esopus, New York, located 96 miles north of New York City. As a child, Truth did not learn to read, although she came to know many parts of the Bible by heart.

When Hardenbergh died in 1806, Truth, who was then

between the ages of six and nine, was sold at auction for $100 with a flock of sheep to John Neely of Kingston, Ulster County. At that time, Truth only spoke Dutch and would indeed continue to speak English with a Dutch accent for the rest of her life. While Neely understood Dutch, his wife did not, leading to miscommunication between Truth and her new mistress. Consequently, Truth experienced many whippings during her time with the Neelys. Truth would later report that Neely treated her cruelly, beating her daily, once even with a bundle of rods. According to Murphy (2011):

> One Sunday morning she was told to go to the barn. On going there, she found her master with a bundle of rods, prepared in the embers and bound together with cords. When he had tied her hands together before her, he gave her the most cruel whipping she was ever tortured with... the scars remain until the present day to testify to the fact. (Murphy, 2011, pp. 4–5)

In 1808, Neely sold Truth for $105 to Martinus Schryver, a tavern keeper from Port Ewen, New York who owned her for 18 months, then sold her in turn to John Dumont of West Park, New York in 1810, who wanted her to work for him as a wool spinner. Her life with Dumont was no better than it had been with Neely as her new master frequently raped her, leading to tension between Truth and his wife, Elizabeth Waring Dumont, who mistreated Truth and made her life even more difficult.

Despite the bleakness of her life at this time, around 1815 Truth met and fell in love with Robert, an enslaved man who worked at a neighboring farm. But Robert's owner, Charles Catton, Jr., did not approve of his slave's relationship with Truth as he did not want his enslaved people to have children with people who were not his slaves as these children would not become his property. One day when Robert snuck over to visit Truth, Catton and his son intercepted him, severely beating him almost to death. Truth and Robert never saw each other again, and Robert died a few years later. This event haunted Truth for the rest of her life.

Truth eventually married an enslaved man named Thomas on an unknown date. He was considerably older than she was and had been married twice before, with at least one of his earlier marriages breaking up because his wife had been sold. Truth also had five children. Her children were: James, who died in childhood, Diana (1815), born as a result of rape by John Dumont, Peter (1821), Elizabeth (1825) and Sophia (c. 1826), the last three of whom were fathered by Thomas. *The Narrative of Sojourner Truth* does not say much about her marriage, while John Dumont's son, Solomon, later recalled that her and Thomas "lived unhappily together" (Horn, 2010, p. 24).

Legislation for the abolition of slavery began in the State

of New York in 1799 with the passing of the Gradual Emancipation Act; however, the process of slave emancipation was not completed until July 4, 1827. This legislation meant that any child born to a slave born after July 4, 1799, was born free, but men were not to be freed before the age of 25 and women the age of 28. It was not until July 4, 1827, that all slaves born before 1799 were freed. Truth's owner, Dumont, had promised her freedom a year before she would be emancipated by the state "if she would do well and be faithful" (Dione, 2020, p. 22). But, when the time came to free her, Dumont failed to keep his promise, claiming that Truth's hand injury had made her less productive and therefore not worthy of freedom.

At this point, Truth made her mind up to leave. In 1826, having spun 100 lb of wool to honor her obligations to Dumont, she left with her infant daughter, Sophia. Because of the emancipation order, she was forced to leave her other children behind. She later recalled: "I did not run off, for I thought that was wicked, but I walked off, believing that to be all right" (Dionne, 2020, p. 22). Truth was emphatic that she had not run away; she had simply left. As she would later tell Dumont: "I did not run away, I walked away by daylight" (National Park Service, 2023a, p. 1).

Truth then walked from her former master's house to New Paltz, New York, where she and her baby were taken in by Isaac and Maria Van Wagenen. The couple did not consider Truth or her baby property; instead, they paid her former master, Dumont, $20 to keep them both. This kind action kept Truth and Sophia safe until the State of New York approved the Emancipation Act one year later.

Truth has the honor of being the first African American woman to win a lawsuit in the United States and to legally fight to reclaim her son's freedom after he had been illegally sold. After she had settled with the Van Wagenen family, Truth found out that her previous owner had sold her six-year-old son, Peter, to Solomon Gedney, who then sent Peter to a plantation owner in Alabama. The Southern States had no emancipation laws which meant that, unless he was rescued, Peter would remain a slave forever. Truth's friends advised her that slaves were not allowed to be sent out of New York State. On this basis, with the aid of the Quakers and using the name Isabella Van Wagenen, Truth filed a lawsuit against Gedney, who still claimed that he owned Peter. On March 15, 1828, the Judge ruled that Gedney had broken the law and Peter must be returned to his mother.

Tragically, Peter was badly traumatized by his experience. His body showed evidence of beatings, and it took some time before he recognized his mother. It is clear that Peter grew into a troubled young man as a result of his childhood trauma. Later, Peter would fall into bad company and began lying to his mother, stealing from his employers, and getting into trouble with the police. Finally, in 1839, Peter shipped out on a Nantucket whaler in order to avoid further trouble, but after sending his mother a few letters, he was never seen again, and it is presumed he was lost at sea.

This was not Truth's last interaction with the law. On another occasion, she was accused by a newspaper of being a witch and of poisoning a leader of a religious group she had been a member of. In 1828, Truth and her son moved to New York City in search of better jobs. There, Truth became increasingly involved in religious organizations, such as the Zion African Church, a woman's evangelical group, and the Magdalene Asylum. At the Magdalene Asylum she met Elijah Pierson, a self-proclaimed minister who believed that he could communicate directly with God. Truth believed she had a similar ability and was mesmerized by Pierson. In August 1831, she moved into Pierson's meetinghouse and became a devout follower of the minister and his religious sect. Along with another mystic, Robert Matthews, who called himself "Matthias," Pierson decided to found a religious community on a farm owned by Benjamin and Ann Folger that was renamed Zion Hill and came to be known as "the Kingdom." However, Truth soon became disillusioned with the Kingdom and left in August 1834. Soon after, a scandal erupted there when the recently deceased Pierson's relatives accused Matthews of poisoning his fellow prophet, despite there being no medical evidence to back up their accusations. Matthews was arrested for murder and a newspaper then implicated Truth in the alleged plot, although she was never charged. Truth responded by suing the newspaper and won a $125 judgment.

On June 1, 1843, Isabella changed her name to Sojourner Truth. She took this name after her conversion to Christianity, justifying her decision on the grounds: "Sojourner because I was to travel up and down the land showing people their sins and being a sign to them, and Truth because I was to declare the truth unto the people" (Library of Congress, 1998, p. 1). Another story says that Truth chose her new name because she heard the Spirit of God telling her to take the name "Sojourner" as part of her calling to preach and that she took the name "Truth" by her own choice to indicate what she would be preaching.

Telling her friends that the spirit of God had told her to leave, she left New York City to travel and preach across America as an itinerant preacher. She clearly made this profound decision on a whim as about an hour before she left, she informed Mrs. Whiting, the woman of the house where she was stopping, that her name was no longer Isabella but Sojourner and that she was going east. When asked why, she replied: "The Spirit calls me there, and I must go" (Horn, 2010, p. 9).

Speeches and Advocacy for Abolition

In 1843, Truth began spreading the word of God at a time where the North was overrun with evangelical movements. Traveling with only a few possessions hastily stuffed into a pillowcase, she journeyed north via the

Connecticut River Valley toward Massachusetts. During this period of her life, Nell Irvin Painter describes Truth as "a singing evangelist whose religion is joyous, optimistic, and at times ecstatic" (Hamilton, 2002b, p. 108). As she traveled, Truth preached beneath big tents at camps set up by Millerites, who believed that the end of the world was near. This led her to attend Millerite Adventist camp meetings. The Millerites were followers of the teachings of William Miller of New York, who preached that Jesus would return to earth in 1843–1844, an act that would lead to the end of the world. Truth's preaching and singing was popular with many members of the Millerite community and her speaking drew large crowds. However, when the anticipated Second Coming did not take place, Truth and many others distanced themselves from the Millerites for a while.

Despite her ultimate rejection of their teachings, the Millerites received Truth warmly and directed her to the Northampton Association, a commune based in Western Massachusetts and run by abolitionists. While there, Truth reported that she enjoyed complete "liberty of thought and speech" (Hamilton, 2002b, p. 108). In 1844, Truth joined the Northampton Association of Education and Industry, based in Florence, Massachusetts. The organization had been founded by abolitionists and supported religious tolerance, women's rights, and pacifism. The Northampton Association operated for four and a half years and welcomed a total of 240 members, with no more than 120 active at any one time. The group lived on a plot of 470 acres where they raised livestock, ran a sawmill, a silk factory, and a gristmill. Truth moved to the community and contributed by overseeing the men and women working in the laundry.

While she was living at the Northampton Association, Truth met Frederick Douglass, William Lloyd Garrison, and David Ruggles, all of whom were prominent figures in the anti-slavery and women's rights movements at that time. Although Douglass later expressed his admiration for Truth's speaking ability, he was initially patronizing of her and saw her as uncultured. This view of Douglass's attitude toward Truth can be gleaned from what he said about her in his article "What I Found at the Northampton Association," written toward the end of his life:

> David Ruggles was not the only colored person who found refuge in this Community. I met here for the first time that strange compound of wit and wisdom, of wild enthusiasm and flint-like common sense, who seemed to feel it her duty to trip me up in my speeches and ridicule my efforts to speak and act like a person of cultivation and refinement. I allude to Sojourner Truth. She was a genuine specimen of the uncultured negro. She cared very little for elegance of speech or refinement of manners. She seemed to please

> herself and others best when she put her ideas in the oddest forms. She was much respected at Florence, for she was honest, industrious, and amiable. Her quaint speeches easily gave her an audience, and she was one of the most useful members of the Community in its day of small things. (Stetson & David, 1994, p. 1848)

While Douglass praised Truth as a useful member of the Northampton Association and a charismatic speaker, Stetson and David (1994) point out that this passage, like much of this particular article, was used to air Douglass's historic grievances against individuals and associations, one of whom appears to have been Truth. Although Truth left no record of her impression of Douglass, she did use her plain talk to challenge him. For example, at an 1852 meeting in Ohio, Douglass spoke of the need for Black people to seize freedom, seemingly by force. When he sat down, Truth rose and asked, "Is God gone?" successfully challenging Douglass's resort to violence and rendering herself as a symbol for faith, non-violence, and God's power to right the wrongs of slavery.

It was at the Northampton Association that Truth became fully involved and acquainted with the abolitionist and women's rights movements. She lived at Northampton for several months before she joined the ranks of the anti-slavery feminists, as the group disbanded in 1846 as it was unable to support itself. Truth did not spend the entirety of the 1843–1850 period involved with religious groups and itinerant preaching. In 1845, she joined the household of George Benson, the brother-in-law of her fellow abolitionist, William Lloyd Garrison, and in 1849 she paid a visit to her daughter and John Dumont before he moved west. At this point, Dumont finally acknowledged the evils of slavery.

Her experiences in the 1840s led Truth to ultimately becoming an abolitionist speaker and crusader for women's rights in the late 1840s. She soon became well-known as an eloquent and passionate speaker, traveling thousands of miles to make powerful speeches against slavery and for women's suffrage. Her career was even more remarkable as it was considered improper for a woman to speak in public at the time.

Truth's appeal to her audiences had something to do with her warm and loving personality. For example, feminist Elizabeth Lukins described Truth in 1851 in the following terms: "Her heart was as soft and loving as a child's, her soul as strong and fixed as the everlasting rocks, and her moral sense has something like inspiration or divination" (Hamilton, 2002b, p. 108). Notably, many of Truth's speeches reflect her background as an itinerant preacher. For example, her opening address to the American Equal Rights Association in 1867 recalls the tone of the prophet Jeremiah, who called on the nation to repent its sins and move forward into a new dispensation:

> If the first woman God ever made was strong enough to turn the world upside down all alone, these women together ought to be able to turn it back, and get it right side up again! And now they is asking to do it, the men better let them. (Bennett, 2005, p. 85)

Here, Truth implies that the arrival of the future dispensation will be the result of women's labors. Thus, it is apparent that Truth's abolitionist and women's rights campaigning was infused with her religious fervor.

Truth's abolitionist work was also promoted by her memoirs and articles written about her by others. She earned some money from her public speaking engagements and also profited from the publication of her *Narrative of Sojourner Truth* (1850), which was written by abolitionist Olive Gilbert and recorded Truth's experiences as a slave. Truth dictated her memoirs to Gilbert and the resulting book was privately published by William Lloyd Garrison. She was able to use the profits from her memoirs to purchase a home in Florence, Massachusetts for $300 and paid off the mortgage on that home in 1854, which was held by her friend Samuel L. Hill, through further memoir sales and those of cartes de visite captioned "I sell the shadow to support the substance."

In the 1850s, Truth met the abolitionist author Harriet Beecher Stowe who, in 1863, wrote about Truth in an article for *Atlantic Monthly* entitled "Sojourner Truth, the Libyan Sibyl" that was a mixture of fact and myth. In her article, Stowe paid tribute to Truth, but she was also condescending of her. For example, when Stowe told about Truth's supposed hymn, she depicted Truth as primitive:

> "There is a holy city"... [Truth] sang with the strong barbaric accent of the native African... Sojourner, singer of the hymn, seemed to impersonate the fervor of Ethiopia, wild savage, hunted of all nations, but burning after God in her tropic heart. (Hamilton, 2002b, p. 108)

This example shows how much publicity Truth received for her abolitionist work at the time but also demonstrates how she was often depicted as somehow primitive and savage compared to her White abolitionist counterparts. It would appear that some of her contemporaries judged her for her lack of education, believing it made her inferior to them in terms of intelligence and outlook.

Intersectionality: Her Fight for Women's Rights and Abolition

Truth's fight for women's rights and abolition can be considered to be an example of intersectionality. This term was coined in 1989 by Professor Kimberlé Williams Crenshaw, a civil rights activist and a critical race legal scholar. According to Crenshaw:

> Intersectionality is a metaphor for understanding the ways that multiple forms of inequality or disadvantage sometimes compound themselves and create obstacles that often are not understood among conventional ways of thinking. (Bates & Patel, 2023, p. 206)

In Truth's case, she was disadvantaged in her own time by both being born a slave and being a woman. Consequently, she was keen to speak to advocate for the rights of both these groups.

Truth spoke out in favor of the rights of African Americans and women, both during and after the Civil War. It is notable that many of her speeches are a mixture of abolitionist and women's rights narratives, generally promoted at events that focused on women's rights.

In many of her speeches, Truth advocated for women's rights. For example, when she spoke before the first national women's rights meeting in Worcester, Massachusetts in 1850, she expanded on her faith in God: "a conviction," she said, "was necessary to bring an end to evil." She also observed that women had: "Set the world wrong by eating the forbidden fruit" but that she would now set it right (Hamilton, 2002b, p. 108). At the women's rights convention in Akron, Ohio, in 1851, Truth asked permission to speak and, according to one reliable report published a month after the speech in *The Anti-Slavery Bugle* by Reverend Maricus Robinson, she said:

> I am a woman's rights. I have as much muscle as any man... I have plowed and reaped and hacked and chopped and mowed and can any man do more than that?... I have heard the Bible and have learned that Eve caused men to sin. Well, if women upset the world, do give her a chance to set it right side up again. (Hamilton, 2002b, p. 108)

According to a later, exaggerated account of the same event, Truth stated these words to the audience and used the phrase "Ain't I a woman?" This famous account of the Akron speech was first published by Frances Gage in 1863, twelve years after Truth had uttered her speech. According to Painter (1996) that account does not hold up, but the essence of the speech remains the same. That is, Truth's words in Akron in 1851 convey a powerful message that, according to the Bible and Truth's own example, women are capable of the same work as men, so women should be afforded equal rights. This speech can be seen as intersectional as here Truth also intended to rebuke those who made women and Black people feel inferior.

It is also clear that her women's rights rhetoric was infused by her experience of slavery. For example, her memoir, as dictated to Gilbert, provides the following reflection on the institution of marriage:

> And what is that religion that sanctions, even by its silence, all that is embraced in the "Peculiar Institution?" If there can be any thing more diametrically opposed to the religion of Jesus than the working of this soul-killing system—which is as truly sanctioned by the religion of America as are her ministers and churches—we wish to be shown where it can be found. (Andrews, 2003, p. 60)

This passage relates to Truth's brief marriage to her husband, Thomas, who had been married twice previously with at least one of the marriages ending because his wife had been sold and taken elsewhere. Gilbert elaborates on this message, pointing out that Thomas would have been encouraged by his master to take a new wife after the sale of each previous one, observing that: "Such is the custom among slaveholders at the present day" (Andrews, 2003, p. 60). Thus, Truth's marriage was not a real marriage as it was almost certainly bigamous, demonstrating how the oppression of her as a young woman was underlined by both slavery and the circumstances of her marriage. Gilbert goes on:

> We have said, Isabella [Truth] was married to Thomas—she was, after the fashion of slavery, one of the slaves performing the ceremony for them; as no true minister of Christ can perform, as in the presence of God, what he knows to be a mere *farce*, a mock marriage, unrecognized by any civil law, and liable to be annulled at any moment, when the interest or caprice of the master should dictate. (Gilbert, cited by Andrews, 2003, p. 60)

As such, Gilbert's memoirs highlight how Truth's experience of marriage highlights the oppressive nature of both slavery and the inferior position of women in society. These passages also help explain how Truth's abolitionist and women's rights campaigning intersect with one another.

Later Life

Around 1857, Truth moved to Battle Creek, Michigan, where she would live for the rest of her life. When the Civil War began in 1861, Truth became increasingly political, agitating for the inclusion of Black people in the Union Army, and then, once they were allowed to join, volunteering for the cause by bringing them clothes and food. Like Harriet Tubman, Truth used her skills as an orator to help recruit Black soldiers to fight for the Union and worked for the National Freedman's Relief Association in Washington, DC, soliciting donations and rallying to provide Black refugees from the South with relief.

Truth's work during the Civil War was so impressive that it earned her an audience with President Abraham Lincoln in October 1864. When she was there, Lincoln showed her a Bible that had been given to him by African Americans in Baltimore. Truth's own account of her visit to the White House tells how she visited with her White friend, Lucy Colman and, although they had to wait some time to see Lincoln in his reception room, both ladies "enjoyed his conversation with others; he showed as much kindness and consideration to the colored persons as the whites—if there was any difference, more" (Coates, 2010, p. 1). Truth concluded her account by stating: "I am proud to say that I never was treated by any one with more kindness and cordiality than were shown to me by that great and good man, Abraham Lincoln" (2010, p. 1).

After the Civil War, Truth focused most of her time and energy on women's suffrage. For example, one of her most famous quotes refers to her campaign to get women the vote and was uttered in New York on May 9, 1867:

> "Now, if you want me to get out of the world, you had better get the women votin' soon. I shan't go till I can do that." (Astin & Leland, 1991, p. 152)

It is apparent that Truth's campaigning for votes for women was an evolution of her campaigning for women's rights. Notably as early as her "Ain't I a Woman" speech in 1851, Truth was keen to emphasize the equality of men and women in the eyes of God:

> Then that little man in Black there, he says women can't have as much rights as men, 'cause Christ wasn't a woman! Where did your Christ come from? Where did Christ come from? From God and a woman! Man had nothing to do with Him." (Schultz & Van Assendelft, 1999, p. 257)

However, she ultimately broke ranks with the woman's suffrage movement's leaders Susan B. Anthony and Elizabeth Cady Stanton after the latter stated that she would not support the Black vote if women were not also given the right.

Even after the civil war, her abolitionist and women's rights activism continued. For example, Truth protested against segregation by riding on Whites-only streetcars in Washington, DC and lobbied Congress to award western lands to the formerly enslaved in order to help them achieve financial independence. Truth campaigned for the latter cause because she saw the 1879 Exodus to Kansas as part of God's divine plan. She also made considerable efforts to find jobs for freed Black Americans struggling with poverty. Furthermore, Truth continued to speak out about a variety of issues, including prison reforms, women's rights, and universal suffrage until the end of her life.

Truth died at a sanatorium in Battle Creek, Michigan on November 26, 1883, aged between 83 and 86. Several thousand mourners attended her funeral, and in December 1883, *The New York Globe* published an obituary of Truth, where it was stated that: "Sojourner Truth stands pre-eminently as the only colored woman who gained a national reputation on the lecture platform in the days before the [Civil] War" (Library of Congress, 1998, p. 1). This observation demonstrates the scope and significance of her achievements.

Truth's Cultural Legacy

Both in her own lifetime and in the modern era, Truth is an inspiration for African Americans and women and continues to have a voice for equal rights that resonates today.

The multiple versions of Truth's speeches have been collected and put together online by The Sojourner Truth Project. The website acknowledges how those who collected Truth's speeches, such as White abolitionist Frances Dana Barker Gage, changed Truth's words and also chose to represent her as having a stereotypical Southern Black slave accent rather than her actual New York

State low-Dutch accent. Such actions were well-intentioned and served the interest of the mid-19th century abolitionist and women's rights movements but, by today's standards, count as an unethical misrepresentation of Sojourner Truth's words and identity. It is also notable that Truth herself disapproved of attempts to alter her words to give the impression that she spoke in the same way as Southern Black slaves. According to an 1851 issue of the *Kalamazoo Daily Telegraph*, Truth prided herself on: "Fairly correct English, which is in all senses a foreign tongue to her... People who report her often exaggerate her expressions, putting into her mouth the most marked Southern dialect, which Sojourner feels is rather taking an unfair advantage of her" (Fitch & Mandziuk, 1997, p. 129). Such acts oversimplify American slave culture and means that most people now no longer appreciate the scope and diversity of America's slave history.

At present, five monuments commemorate the life of Sojourner Truth, located in various parts of the United States. There is the Sojourner Truth Monument at Battle Creek, Michigan; the Sojourner Truth Memorial Statue in Florence, Massachusetts; two further statues in San Diego and Sacramento, California; and she is also honored on the Monument to Women's Suffrage in New York City. The existence of these monuments shows how the life and example of Sojourner Truth are worthy of being remembered.

Chapter Four
Elizabeth Heyrick
Mother of Immediatism

This chapter explores the life of Elizabeth Heyrick, a British writer and activist who became involved in the anti-slavery movement in the early 1820s. She was a member of the Birmingham Ladies Society for the Relief of Negro Slaves and later founded the Leicester Ladies' Anti-Slavery Society in 1825.

Heyrick was a passionate and outspoken advocate for the immediate and unconditional abolition of slavery, and her writings and speeches were influential in the abolitionist movement. She discussed her advocacy for immediate and unconditional abolition in her influential 1824 pamphlet *Immediate, Not Gradual Abolition; or, an Inquiry Into the Shortest, Safest, and Most Effectual Means of Getting Rid of West India Slavery*. Here Heyrick argued that slavery was a moral abomination that could not be gradually phased out. The pamphlet criticized the policy developed by the predominantly male leadership of the Anti-Slavery Society. Here she declared that immediate abolition "is the only solid foundation on which the reformation of the slave, and the still more needful reformation of his usurping masters can be built" (Harmer, 2001, p. 77). Although the leadership of the Anti-Slavery Society attempted to repress Elizabeth's views, her arguments were supported by women's abolitionist groups. Her pamphlet was widely circulated and helped to shift public opinion toward the abolitionist cause.

Heyrick also played a key role in organizing the National Anti-Slavery Convention of 1830, which brought together abolitionists from across Britain and helped to solidify the movement's commitment to immediate abolition. Her activism continued throughout her life, and she remained a prominent figure in the British abolitionist movement until her death in 1831.

As a British woman primarily operating in the United Kingdom, at first glance an examination of Elizabeth's life in a book where all the other women are American might appear out of place. However, she is included for the very good reason that her contributions shaped and fashioned later developments in the American abolitionist movement. Also, this book explores the abolitionist movement in the Industrialized nations across the Atlantic, not just America.

Like many benevolent institutions and causes that began in the United States in the early 19th century, the anti-slavery or abolitionist movement was fashioned and developed according to British models. Thus, on the whole, the American abolitionist movement mimicked the British anti-slavery movement, borrowing from its tactics and symbols as well as looking to its leaders, such as George Thompson, for approval and advice. Elizabeth's contributions were particularly influential in the United States due to the significance of her pamphlet *Immediate, Not Gradual Abolition* on the American abolitionist movement. Therefore, her inclusion here is very much justified.

Early Life

Elizabeth was born on December 4, 1769, in Leicester, the second of five children born to John Coltman (1727–1808) and his wife, Elizabeth Cartwright. Her father worked in the textile industry as a producer of worsted cloth, while her mother was a craftswoman, poet, and book reviewer. John Coltman was a successful worsted hosiery manufacturer and a leading figure in the only large-scale industry in Leicester, as well as a dedicated scholar, antiquary, and supporter of political reform. Meanwhile, Elizabeth's mother was an accomplished artist and poet who corresponded with a network of literary men associated with her relative, the London publisher and writer Robert Dodsley.

Both her parents were dissenters, meaning that they objected to the Anglican religion. Instead, the family were Unitarians but converted to Methodism following a visit to the family home by the popular Methodist minister, John Wesley. The Coltmans were radical dissenters influenced by Enlightenment thought. This subset in the dissenting movement developed an image of a more benevolent God and stressed religion's importance of benevolence toward one's fellow human beings. Toward the end of the 18th century, rational dissent became identified with political radicalism, and the ethics of benevolence were extended to support the rights of man at the time of the American and French Revolutions. This background appears to have inspired Elizabeth's later scholarship and radicalism, as her activism and concern for others less fortunate than herself was apparent from a young age. For example, as a child, she chose the plainest kitten from a litter, claiming that it needed to be saved the most.

As a young woman, Elizabeth worked as a schoolteacher until she married John Heyrick on March 10, 1787. At the time of their marriage, John was working as Leicester's town clerk, but shortly after he married Elizabeth, he joined the 15th Regiment of Light Dragoons and left Leicester to serve in England and Ireland, accompanied by Elizabeth. However, tragedy struck in 1795 when John died of angina while Elizabeth was at church. There were no children from the marriage, which was said to have been stormy, although Elizabeth was devastated by her husband's death and never remarried.

After her husband's death, Elizabeth returned to Leicester, moving back in with her parents and leaving the Methodists to join the Society of Friends, familiarly known as the Quakers, renouncing all pleasures, and taking to social reform. She also became a follower of Thomas Paine, and inspired by him, became a prison visitor and campaigned against bull-baiting, which involved a bull being led to a stake in the ground and attacked by dogs. In her lifetime, up to 20 of her books and pamphlets were published, addressing a range of social issues such as the Corn Laws, vagrancy legislation, corporal punishment, prison reform, animal welfare, and the plight of the industrial poor. She wrote many more, but these went unpublished. Her writings reflect the breadth of her learning. For example, having read the works of the English economist David Ricardo and admired the radical Luddites' smashing of industrial machinery, Elizabeth extended their thought to forge connections between political economy and systematic systems of oppression, like slavery. It was through making this link that the philosophy of immediatism was born.

Elizabeth also engaged in direct action as part of her social reform campaigning. On one occasion, she stopped a bull-baiting contest by buying the bull and hiding it in the parlor of a nearby cottage until the crowd dispersed. On another occasion, she made an effort to experience the life of Irish migrant workers by living in a shepherd's cottage and only eating potatoes. Elizabeth also agitated for labor rights in conjunction with abolition, fighting for fair wages and safer working conditions. Additionally, she visited prisons and argued against war and capital punishment. In other words, Elizabeth was a woman who devoted every moment of her life to social causes and social reform.

Role in the British Abolitionist Movement

Although Elizabeth championed many social issues and reforms, her main focus was the abolition of slavery in the British colonies. In this, she may have been inspired by the example of her elder brother, Samuel Coltman, who was a member of the original abolition movement in the 1790s. Also, her father was a political radical and a supporter of the campaign against the slave trade. She may have also been inspired by the ideas of the Unitarian movement. The Unitarians believed that the only major difference between the sexes was man's capacity for physical force. For this reason, they felt that there was no natural reason why women should not use their abilities for intellectual and moral growth to bring about social progress. Consequently, her Unitarian faith alongside her upbringing in a family of rational dissenters gave Elizabeth the impetus to campaign against slavery.

Also, Elizabeth's anti-slavery activism was encouraged by her involvement in The Anti-Slavery Society, which existed between 1823 and 1839 and was dedicated to the elimination of slavery in the British Empire. At the time Elizabeth was active, despite the fact that England had banned the British Atlantic slave trade in 1808, people were still allowed to own slaves in its colonies. She believed that slavery was something "in which all are implicated; we are all guilty" (British Library, 2023a, p. 1). The Anti-Slavery Society was led by Thomas Clarkson (1760–1846) and William Wilberforce (1759–1833). The society was divided into two groups of campaigners: Those in favor of gradual abolition of slavery and those who championed more immediate action. When she joined the group in 1824, Elizabeth quickly became part of the latter group. It is also notable that Elizabeth's radicalism in the slavery movement was far greater compared to that of her brothers, who also supported the anti-slavery cause but took a far more cautious position toward domestic reform and anti-slavery.

Elizabeth's most successful pamphlet was *Appeal to the Hearts and Consciences of British Women* (1828), with 1,500 copies of the pamphlet being bought by the Anti-Slavery Society for distribution in 1828–1829 (British Library, 2023b). She also felt that women had an integral role to play in promoting abolitionism. To this end, she directly appealed for women to join the anti-slavery movement. Aware of the important role women played in running the home at the time, she felt that abolitionist campaigning was an extension of the transitional role of women and could be used strategically to promote the cause. Thus, abolitionist women were encouraged to use their position as homemakers to promote boycotting of products produced through slavery while women's groups attempted to pressure men to seek the immediate rather than gradual abolition of slavery. As such, women's anti-slavery efforts in 19th century Britain were constructed in a way to support those undertaken by men.

During the 1820s and 1830s, female campaigners played an increasingly prominent role in the fight for abolition, setting up ladies' anti-slavery associations in towns and cities across the United Kingdom. Women's anti-slavery campaigning activities included petitioning, producing informative pamphlets, door-to-door canvassing, fundraising, and encouraging abstention from slave-produced sugar. The purpose of activities such as house-to-house canvassing was to sell and distribute anti-slavery pamphlets. These were sold to the well-off and lent to the poor. Such activities were unusual for women at the time as they were traditionally discouraged from becoming involved in politics; however, they could not campaign on the same terms as men as they were excluded from campaigning in Parliament.

Such restrictions on women's campaigning activities did not deter Elizabeth. With her friend Susannah Watts (1768–1842) and other female campaigners, Elizabeth canvassed Leicester, promoting the boycott of sugar and other goods produced by enslaved labor. Elizabeth and Susannah had a long-standing friendship, with Susannah having taught French at the school where Elizabeth worked. The two women engaged in door-to-door campaigning to encourage their neighbors to stop buying sugar produced by slave plantations following the publication of *Immediate, Not Gradual Abolition* in the 1820s. For example, in June 1825, Elizabeth and Susannah publicly declared their campaign to encourage the citizens of Leicester to boycott sugar produced by slaves: "In the Town of Leicester, by the zeal and activity of a very few individuals alone, nearly one fourth of the population viz. 1,500 families have been so impressed by the subject, as to engage themselves to abstain from the use of West-Indian sugar" (Story of Leicester, 2023, p. 1).

This action was part of Elizabeth's campaign to encourage her fellow citizens to quit using and grocers selling sugar produced by slave labor in the West Indies. Instead, Elizabeth encouraged people to ensure that any sugar they bought was grown in Britain's colonies in the East Indies, such as Malaya (modern-day Malaysia) and Bengal (a state in India), where cane-field laborers were impoverished but technically free. To aid the campaign, Elizabeth wrote a series of booklets. In one of these broadsides, she asked those who favored the gradual emancipation of slaves to ponder whether "greater victories have been achieved by the combined expression of individual opinion than by fleets and armies; that greater moral revolutions have been accomplished by the combined exertions of individual resolution than were ever affected by acts of Parliament" (Zoellner, 2020, p. 1).

Elizabeth also urged householders to ensure that they did not purchase any produce that was the result of slave labor as, she believed, that such a boycott could successfully end slavery. As a solution, she proposed that: "Instead of purchasing that luxury, the cultivation of which constitutes at once the chief profits and oppressions of slavery, they can substitute that which is the genuine produce of free labor" (Tinubu, 2018, p. 1). Furthermore, she described the West Indian planters as thieves and those who bought their produce as receivers of stolen goods. In her boycott, Elizabeth was aided by her friend Susannah Watts, Lucy Townsend, Mary Lloyd, Sarah Wedgwood, and Sophia Sturge. She also visited all the grocers in Leicester to urge them not to stock slave-owner produced goods. However, her focus on citizen-driven change through consumer activism was unpopular with most of her contemporaries who favored a government-driven effort to eradicate slavery.

Elizabeth and her fellow boycotters deployed different tactics to educate rich and poor citizens about the need to boycott West Indian sugar. For example, the pamphlet *What Does Your Sugar Cost? A Cottage Conversation on the Subject of British Negro Slavery* was intended for a poorer audience and distributed in the thousands. It was written in a conversational style and tone and told the story of a lady coming to a home to convince the mother and daughter of the house to stop consuming sugar produced by slaves. This work was meant to be accessible, to appeal to audiences with less education, and to provide an easy template for ladies to use while canvassing. However, another pamphlet, *Reasons for Substituting East Indian*

Sugar was written with an upper-class audience in mind. Instead of the comfortable discussion found in the previous pamphlet, the latter work focused on discussion of the subject in Parliament. Pamphlets were even written for children to educate them about the sugar boycott, such as one by Charlotte Townsend entitled *Pity the Negro or, an Address to the Children on the Subject of Slavery*.

Elizabeth was instrumental in the formation of the Female Society for Birmingham and the Leicester Ladies' Anti-Slavery Society. The society began with a meeting held at the home of Lucy Townsend on April 8, 1825, to discuss the role of women in the anti-slavery movement. The women at the meeting, which included Elizabeth, Mary Lloyd, Sophia Sturge, and Sarah Wedgwood, decided to form the Birmingham Ladies Society for the Relief of Negro Slaves (later renamed the Female Society for Birmingham). The purpose of the group was to promote the sugar boycott, target shops and shoppers, distribute pamphlets, visit homes, draw petitions, and call meetings on abolitionism. At the inaugural meeting of the group, Elizabeth was appointed treasurer and, due to her influence, a Leicester branch of the same society was formed a month later.

From its formation, the Female Society for Birmingham remained independent from both the national Anti-Slavery Society and the local men's Anti-Slavery Society. In fact, the society acted as the center of an evolving national network of female anti-slavery societies instead of as a local auxiliary. The group also fostered international connections and received publicity for its actions in Benjamin Lundy's abolitionist periodical *The Genius of Universal Emancipation*. As such, the group influenced the formation of female anti-slavery societies in the United States. It also inspired the setting up of similar groups across the United Kingdom in cities such as Nottingham, Leicester, Sheffield, Glasgow, Norwich, London, and Chelmsford. By 1831, a total of 73 such female-led organizations had been set up to campaign against slavery. The Female Society for Birmingham also made contact with like-minded women in Ireland and the United States. These groups became an influential force in the abolition movement, particularly through encouraging a shift toward campaigning for immediate abolition.

"Immediate, Not Gradual Abolition"

Of all of Elizabeth's efforts to eradicate slavery, her best remembered contribution to the abolitionist movement is the publication of her 1824 pamphlet *Immediate, Not Gradual Abolition; or, an Inquiry Into the Shortest, Safest, and Most Effectual Means of Getting Rid of West India Slavery*. The pamphlet was published anonymously in London, with second and third editions published the same year, and it was inspired by a rebellion by slaves in the British colony of Demerara on August 18, 1823.

Like her campaign to boycott consumer goods produced by slavery, the pamphlet came about as a result of Elizabeth's contempt for male abolitionists in Parliament, who she believed continued to condone slavery for economic reasons. She believed that key early-19th century male anti-slavery campaigners such as William Wilberforce and Thomas Clarkson were too "polite" and "accommodating" of enslavers (Heyrick, 1824, p. 14). Wilberforce and Clarkson both promoted the idea that the abolition of the slave trade was the step toward the gradual end of slavery in the British colonies as slaves could no longer be replaced. However, by the 1820s it was obvious that this had not happened as slavery still flourished, many years after the trade had ceased.

Instead, Elizabeth realized that a strategy apart from the gradualist approach was needed in order to eliminate slavery for good. Her approach is known as immediatism, which was to become a key tenet of radical abolitionist philosophy. It promoted the belief that emancipation, when effected, should be immediate rather than gradual. To this end, Elizabeth advocated that the abolition of slavery should not be associated with any form of compensated emancipation for slaveholders or with the removal of emancipated Black people through any colonization scheme. From this perspective, as slavery was inherently evil, it was unacceptable for gradualists to oppose slavery but actively work to prolong its effects. While some feared that, in light of the recent slave rebellion in Demerara, the immediate abolition of slavery would result in insurrection, Elizabeth sympathized with the rebels saying, "it was not in the case of self-defense from the most degrading, intolerable oppression" (Bownas, 2020, p. 41).

She promoted her strategy in a variety of ways. For example, during the general election of 1826, Elizabeth asked people to only vote for candidates that supported the immediate freeing of slaves. She highlighted her message by quoting a letter she received from a woman living in Wiltshire. That woman told her:

> Men may propose only gradually to abolish the worst of crimes... but why should we countenance such enormities? We must not talk of gradually abolishing murder, licentiousness, cruelty, tyranny. (Hochschild, 2005, p. 326)

Such stunts complemented the message she promoted in *Immediate, Not Gradual Abolition*. There, she emphasized that a campaign of gradual mitigation and abolition was doomed to fail due to the vested interests of the slave owners.

She concluded that "the spirit of accommodation and conciliation has been the spirit of delusion" as slavery was so entrenched in everyday life (McCone, 2021, p. 1). For example, the wealth of slavery and its promoters formed part of the political establishment, while its products were widely sold and distributed. The latter was the motivation behind the sugar boycott. Believing that slavery was inherently evil, Elizabeth therefore saw that there was no other option than to fight against it in a spirit of holy war, using every means available.

These arguments were explored and justified in *Immediate, Not Gradual Abolition*. Notably, the frontispiece of the pamphlet shows a slave standing in defiance, an echo of the best-selling Wedgwood medallion where a slave is depicted humbly kneeling. The latter slave utters the question, "Am I not a man and a brother?" While on Elizabeth's pamphlet, the slave asserts "I am a man, your brother." The content of the pamphlet was even more radical. Therein, Elizabeth pointed out that although the slave trade had been abolished, the trade and slavery still, in practice, continued, demonstrating how she had broken from the policy of gradually ending slavery promoted by the mainstream abolition movement. Instead, she used her platform to promote direct action, such as the sugar boycott, arguing that if just 10% of the British population gave up sugar, this would defeat the slave interest.

Elizabeth also used the pamphlet to attack the "slow, cautious, accommodating measures" adopted by the leaders of the anti-slavery movement in Britain. She expanded on this point, stating:

> The perpetuation of slavery in our West India colonies is not an abstract question, to be settled between the government and the

planters; it is one in which we are all implicated, we are all guilty of supporting and perpetuating slavery. The West Indian planter and the people of this country stand in the same moral relation to each other as the thief and receiver of stolen goods. (Simkin, 1997, p. 1)

Although Elizabeth's approach to ending slavery was radical, she was not the first woman to propose a boycott of products produced by slaves. Hannah More, a celebrated writer and leader of the 18th-century Blue Stockings Society, a movement of female intellectuals, had in 1788 proposed to a friend that they should "taboo" the use of slave-made West Indian sugar (McCone, 2021, p. 1). This idea rapidly evolved into the 1791–1792 boycott campaign, in which around 300,000 individuals partook in the rejection of West Indian sugar, many of whom were housewives.

Immediate, Not Gradual Abolition was widely popular, and the pamphlet was widely distributed at anti-slavery meetings across the United Kingdom in the 1820s. Twelve pamphlets were bought by the Anti-Slavery Committee for use by its members, although those who were aware that the then-anonymous author was a woman, disapproved of Elizabeth's stance as too masculine or unwomanly, with gendered rhetoric used to undermine her contribution to the anti-slavery debate.

Elizabeth's demands for the immediate abolition of slavery also went against the attitudes of the leadership of the Anti-Slavery Society, as they promoted gradual abolition, an approach attacked by Elizabeth as "slow, cautious, accommodating" (Simkin, 1997, p. 1). For this reason, the leadership of the Anti-Slavery Society attempted to suppress information about the existence of the pamphlet, with William Wilberforce giving out instructions that leaders of the movement were not to speak about it at women's Anti-Slavery Society gatherings. He also opposed the militant behavior of some of the women involved in the abolition movement.

However, not all of the male leaders of the Anti-Slavery Society agreed with Wilberforce's opinions regarding the active involvement of women in the abolitionist cause. For example, in a letter to Anne Knight dated November 14, 1834, George Stephen acknowledged that the energy of the female members of the movement was vital to its success. He stated that:

> [The] Ladies Associations did everything... They circulated publications; they procured the money to publish; they talked, coaxed and lectured: they got up public meetings and filled our halls and platforms when the day arrived; they carried round petitions and enforced the duty of signing them... In a word, they formed the cement of the whole

> anti-slavery building—without their aid we never should have kept waiting. (Simkin, 1997, p. 1)

Thomas Clarkson, William Wilberforce's fellow leader in the anti-slavery movement, was also much more sympathetic of women than his contemporary, believing that women should have a full education and access to public life, even writing to Elizabeth's friend Lucy Townsend lamenting that "very little attention is paid to their [women's] opinions" (Wilson, 1989, p. 91). Furthermore, 10% of the financial supporters of the Anti-Slavery Society were women, and in some areas, such as Manchester, over a quarter of the organization's subscribers were women.

Ultimately, it is apparent that *Immediate, Not Gradual Abolition* was influential in shifting public opinion to support the abolitionist cause. Despite Wilberforce ordering the leaders of Anti-Slavery Societies across Britain not to discuss it, it was discussed at meetings all over the country. The pamphlet also appeared to have "given women permission to speak" as it led to the formation of over 70 female anti-slavery societies across the country, all of which supported Elizabeth's immediatist approach (Miller, 2021, p. 1). In April 1830, the Female Society for Birmingham submitted a motion to the National Conference of the Anti-Slavery Society calling for a campaign to immediately end slavery in the British colonies. Elizabeth further proposed that women's associations should withdraw their £50 funding to the Anti-Slavery Society if it did not support the resolution. Due to the fact that the Female Society of Birmingham was one of the largest donors to the Anti-Slavery Society and influenced donations made by other ladies' associations, this action could have seriously undermined the work of the Anti-Slavery Society. Consequently, at its May 1830 conference, the Anti-Slavery Society agreed to drop the words "gradual abolition" from its title and support the campaign for the immediate end of slavery.

Elizabeth's pamphlet was even discussed in Parliament, where it caused a stir as its vigorous style made many think that it was the work of a man rather than that of a woman. In fact, when it came to be discussed in Parliament, *Immediate, Not Gradual Abolition* was described as "the work of some gentleman" due to its fiery tone (James & Shuttleworth, 2017, p. 49).

Collaboration with American Abolitionists

Elizabeth used her Quaker connections to distribute *Immediate, Not Gradual Abolition* in the United States. The pamphlet was first published in America in 1825 after it was picked up by Quaker abolitionist Benjamin Lundy and circulated through Quaker communities. It was reprinted and published in serial installments, starting in November 1825 in Lundy's anti-slavery paper the *Genius of Universal Emancipation*. The pamphlet was then reprinted in Boston and Philadelphia and sold thousands of copies in the United States. It soon became clear that the immediatist philosophy was popular in the United States and, due to its popularity, several editions were published in the 1830s, including ones in 1836, 1837, and 1838.

Elizabeth's anti-slavery campaigning was warmly admired in the United States, particularly by a number of prominent American abolitionists including William Lloyd Garrison, Frederick Douglass, Benjamin Lundy, and Lucretia Mott. In particular, Mott admired Elizabeth's work as it promoted women's participation in public life and social reform, while Garrison praised her on his visit to Britain in 1840 at a speech he gave in Glasgow.

In America, Elizabeth's pamphlet was published in her name rather than anonymously, and it contained further information concerning its impact in Britain and on the leaders of the Anti-Slavery Society. Notably, several American editions of *Immediate, Not Gradual Abolition* state that it:

> Proved greatly advantageous to the cause of Emancipation in the British West Indies. Until this time, Wilberforce, and the other leading abolitionists in Great Britain, had directed all their energy towards the Abolition of the Slave Trade... This pamphlet changed their views, they now attacked slavery as a sin to be forsaken immediately and the result is

known. (DeHart, 2020, p. 1)

Thus, in the United States, Elizabeth's contributions to abolitionism received far more praise than they ever had in Britain. Furthermore, her written work and activism had a profound impact on the activism of American abolitionists right up until the American Civil War.

Lasting Impact

After the publication of *Immediate, Not Gradual Abolition*, Elizabeth published several more anti-slavery pamphlets, some of which specifically addressed women. She was also greatly admired in the Midlands, where she lived. Her writing was also popular among women. However, over the years, Elizabeth became despondent that her abolitionist campaigning seemed to have done little to facilitate any real change. On December 28, 1826, depressed about her lack of success in getting slavery abolished, she wrote to Lucy Townsend: "Nothing human can dispel that despairing torpor into which I have been plunging deeper and deeper for many months past" (Simkin, 1997, p. 1). Elizabeth died on October 18, 1831, and thus did not live to see the passing of the Abolition of Slavery Act in 1833.

Her friend, Susannah Watts, took up the baton of Elizabeth's work, continuing to steadfastly campaign against slavery. Just before slavery was entirely eliminated throughout the British Colonies from August 1, 1834, Susannah was involved in collecting local signatures for the London Female Anti-Slavery Society's national petition. Also, Elizabeth's role in bringing about the eradication of slavery was not forgotten by her contemporaries. At an 1833 speech in Glasgow, the American abolitionist William Lloyd Garrison praised Elizabeth in the following terms:

> Who first gave the world the doctrine of immediate emancipation? It was a woman of England—Elizabeth Heyrick. Mrs. Heyrick was the highly respected, talented, and uncompromising friend of liberty... (Story of Leicester, 2023, p. 1)

In 1862, a *Brief Sketch* of her life was anonymously published, probably by her niece Alicia Cooper, which described Elizabeth as "one of the noblest pioneers of social liberty, not only for her own sex, but for mankind at large" (Grundy, 2010, p. 1)

Despite the respect and admiration Elizabeth received from her contemporaries for her work, not many people know much about her and her efforts to abolish slavery today. Grundy (2010) notes that Elizabeth was barely mentioned by the media during the 2007 celebrations for the bicentenary of the British abolition of slavery. However, Shirley Aucutt did a brief biography of Elizabeth. It was only in Leicester, where she lived for most of her life, that an exhibition of her life and works was hosted.

Such attitudes may stem from the lack of acknowledgement of the contributions of Elizabeth and other women to the anti-slavery movement in her lifetime. For example, despite her extensive work for the abolitionist cause, *The Anti-Slavery Reporter* only named Elizabeth once in January 1828 and did not carry a notice of her death. As was the case with ladies' anti-slavery societies in general, women's contributions to the abolitionist movement in Britain were ignored rather than celebrated.

Although Elizabeth has been nearly lost to history, with this book we revive her and her amazing contributions to the abolitionist cause.

Chapter Five
Mary Ann Shadd Cary
Champion of Change

Mary Ann Shadd Cary (1823–1893) was one impressive woman. She was a Canadian journalist, teacher, and lawyer who was a vocal advocate for abolition and women's suffrage. She was born in Delaware, Canada West (now Ontario), in 1823 and was the first Black female newspaper publisher and editor in North America. She also traveled to the United States to give speeches in support of abolition and worked with the Underground Railroad to help enslaved people escape to freedom. She was known for saying: "We should do more and talk less." After the Civil War, Mary Ann became involved in the women's suffrage movement and was a prominent voice for women's rights. She was the first Black woman to attend law school in the United States, graduating from Howard University Law School aged 60 in 1883 to become the second ever Black woman lawyer. She worked throughout her life. Mary Ann's legacy as an abolitionist and a trailblazer for Black women's rights has been celebrated by many, and she remains an important figure in the history of the abolitionist movement.

Safe Haven

Mary Ann Shadd Cary was born Mary Ann Camberton Shadd on October 9, 1823, in Wilmington, Delaware as the eldest of the 13 children of Abraham Doras Shadd and Harriet Parnell, both of whom were abolitionists who often sheltered fugitive slaves. Abraham was a shoemaker and a leader among Delaware's free Black community, and Harriet was originally from North Carolina. Although Mary Ann's family were free Black people, she was born at a time where thousands of Black Americans were still enslaved in the nation's Southern states. Also, as a Black woman, she was part of one of America's most marginalized groups.

Free Black society at that time was diverse but economically and socially stratified. Some people, like most of the Shadd family, had been free for several generations and thus had access to economic and social opportunities, such as opening businesses or accessing education. However, others were still enslaved or had been more recently enslaved and therefore had less opportunities for education and self-improvement than Mary Ann and her family. The Shadd family felt these differences acutely and did everything they could to improve the situation, despite facing discrimination and segregation, even as free Black people living in the North.

The Shadds seemed like a typical middle-class free Black

family to their neighbors, but they had a secret. Abraham and Harriet were, like the subject of Chapter 1, Harriet Tubman, part of the Underground Railroad, as their home was a stop on the secret network. Before the Civil War, slavery was legal in Delaware; although, by 1850, almost 90% of the African American population in the state was not enslaved, and Wilmington was an important transfer point for escaped enslaved people fleeing North for freedom. Being involved in the Underground Railroad was risky and dangerous work that could incur large fines or attacks by angry enslavers. Mary Ann's parents decided to take such huge risks as they sincerely believed in abolitionism. Her parents' commitment to what they believed in later inspired Mary Ann to take action to change the world herself.

When Mary Ann was 10-years-old, the state of Delaware passed a law that limited the ability of Black children to attend school. Delaware never passed a law against the instruction of Black people, but in 1833 it did introduce an Act fining every person who sold a slave out of state or brought one into the state. From each of these penalties, $5 went into a school fund for White children alone, thereby limiting Black children's access to education. In 1833, Abraham and Harriet moved the family to West Chester, Pennsylvania, where they continued their work with the Underground Railroad. Here, Mary Ann was able to pursue her education at a Quaker-sponsored school.

Although Pennsylvania was a free state, Mary Ann and

her family experienced continuous segregation and discrimination that made daily life challenging. The situation the family found themselves in was usual for their time and place. For example, at the time, most educational facilities in the Northern United States where slavery was mainly banned were segregated with Black and White children educated separately from each other. Such discrimination only deepened the Shadd family's commitment to the cause for equality for all Black Americans. Around this time, Abraham was elected president of the National Convention for the Improvement of Free People of Color in Philadelphia.

After Mary Ann completed her education at the age of 16, she became a teacher in her native Wilmington and opened a school for Black children. As a young woman, Mary Ann began to closely follow the anti-slavery movement in the United States but became frustrated that their leaders constantly talked about the need to end slavery when nothing seemed to change. In 1848, Frederick Douglass asked readers of the abolitionist newspaper *The North Star* to write in and share what could be done to improve the lives of all Black Americans. Mary Ann replied, "We should do more and talk less" (Women and the American Story, 2023b, p. 1). Douglass published the letter, and it was the first time that Mary Ann was featured in print. Her statement was blunt and forward thinking, qualities that would be hallmarks of her later career as an activist.

Mary Ann's life changed drastically in 1850 after Congress passed the Fugitive Slave Act on September 18 0f that year, which made it illegal for any person to help an enslaved person escape their enslaver, regardless of where they lived. The Act levied heavy penalties on anyone who refused to comply. The new law also made it easier for slave catchers to capture free Black Americans and sell them into slavery. Abolitionist newspapers attacked the Fugitive Slave Act as a violation of American rights, as the new law did not make sense because, according to the Act, those living in the mainly free Northern states should be punished for harboring runaways. It also meant that the free states were no longer a safe haven for Black people, with an estimated 15,000–20,000 fleeing to Canada after the Act was passed between the fall of 1850 and 1860 (Norton et al., 2015; Horton & Horton, 2005). By 1861, there were an estimated 40,000 Black citizens living in Canada, including those who had escaped slavery in America (Cunningham, 2016).

Having spent the previous decade teaching in various towns and cities on the Eastern Seaboard of the United States, including Norristown, Pennsylvania; Trenton, New Jersey; and New York City, Mary Ann decided that it was no longer safe to live in the United States, so with her brother Issac, she moved to Ontario, Canada. She had visited Canada West in 1850 to research the proposal of Black emigration to Canada and moved there in 1851.

Mary Ann decided to emigrate to Canada after attending the first North American Convention of Colored

Freemen held at St. Lawrence Hall in Toronto on September 10, 1851. The event was presided over by Josiah Henson, Henry Bibb, and J.T. Fisher, and other prominent figures attended alongside hundreds of leaders from the Black communities in Canada, England, and the United States. Many of the delegates attending the convention encouraged enslaved Americans and refugees to flee enslavement by moving to Canada in the wake of the recent Fugitive Slave Act. Mary Ann was persuaded to follow this course of action after meeting activists and publishers of the newspaper *Voice of the Fugitive*, Henry and Mary Bibb, at the meeting, who offered her a teaching position near their home in Sandwich, Canada West.

Mary Ann and Isaac were soon joined by their parents and the rest of the family. Mary Ann believed the move to be a political one as it gave her and her family more freedom to continue fighting for abolitionism across the border. During the 1850s, she lived in Windsor, Chatham, and Ontario respectively, eventually becoming a Canadian citizen in 1862.

The Dominion of Canada was not created until 1867. Instead, the country we now know as Canada was divided into Canada West (modern-day Ontario), Canada East (modern-day southern Quebec), New Brunswick, Nova Scotia, and Prince Edward Island. Slavery had been abolished in Canada in 1831, and the rest of the British Commonwealth nations followed on July 26, 1833. These events resulted in Canada and the British Caribbean Islands becoming magnets for freedom seekers from the United States. Canada was especially attractive in this regard as it had always stood up for the rights of escaped slaves. For example, in the 1830s, Canada had refused to extradite freedom seekers Lucie and Thornton Blackburn and, since then, several others.

Many of the Black people that made their way to Canada were recent runaways, but some fugitives, among them Mary Ann and her family, were longtime residents of the free states who feared for their safety if they remained in America. In this venture, they were encouraged by free and escaped Black people who had already settled in Canada. For example, in 1851, Henry Bibb, who had escaped slavery in Kentucky in the 1840s and had established Canada's first Black newspaper, *The Voice of the Fugitive,* in Sandwich Township, Ontario, in his editorials urged African Americans to come north to experience true freedom in Canada. Furthermore, in the spring of 1852 as a way of incentivizing Black people, he reported that "[Canada's] Underground Railroad is doing good business this spring" (Horton & Horton, 2005, p. 155).

Many Black people in Pennsylvania in particular, where Mary Ann and her family had lived for the previous 17 years, decided to leave for Canada rather than remain in the United States. Notably, communities in southern Pennsylvania, close to the South and the most vulnerable to slaveholders, lost substantial proportions of their Black populations during the 1850s. For example, the

African American population of Columbia, Pennsylvania decreased by more than half in a matter of months, while *The Liberator* reported that in Pittsburgh "nearly all the waiters in the hotels [had] fled to Canada" (Horton & Horton, 2005, p. 155).

Mary Ann became an advocate of immigration. In 1852, she wrote an article encouraging other Black Americans to make the journey north to Canada. To this end, she published several pamphlets and articles that presented Canada as a safe haven for both free Black people and former slaves. For example, in her pamphlet *A Plea for Emigration; or, Notes of Canada West* (1852), Mary Ann told Black Americans where they should settle in Canada, what they could expect when they got there, and encouraged them to take the journey north. In that pamphlet, Mary Ann also described Canada West's temperate climate, excellent society, and agricultural yields as well as Canada's familiar yet more accepting culture. She expressed her certainty that in this fertile area, just north of Lake Erie, hard work would be rewarded with economic independence.

Mary Ann promoted Canada as a safe haven for former slaves and free Black people on the basis that it had common cultural links with the United States in terms of language and religion, as well as political, social, and economic organization. To this end, she promoted Canada as the best place for Black settlement and pushed for the integration of Black people into British Canadian society, also denouncing racial separation in any form. Such views were controversial as they challenged both current segregationist practices in larger society and Black nationalist views about how communities should be constructed. Interestingly, Mary Ann's approach to Black integration in Canada reflects W.E.B. DuBois' later notion of the existence of a "double consciousness" among Black people as they struggled within a system dominated by Western and Eurocentric institutions. Mary Ann's approach also ultimately led to tensions between herself and other members of the Black community in Canada, as demonstrated in the next section.

Opening the Door

After her arrival in Canada, Mary Ann set up a racially integrated school for Black refugees that was open to all children who could afford to attend and was funded by financial support from the American Missionary Association. However, this venture led to a falling out between Mary Ann and Henry and Mary Bibb, who favored segregation, leading to a series of furious editorials between the two that were published in *Voice of the Fugitive*. This led to Mary Ann losing her funding for the school and her teaching job.

It is notable that scholar Shirley J. Yee (1997) believes that Mary Ann's activism was more about securing a place for herself in the Black movement of the day rather than finding a new geographic location for Black people escaping slavery. This perspective may make sense in light of her later actions.

The end of her new school in Canada was a personal setback to Mary Ann, but it did have one positive outcome in the sense that it led her to turn her talents to journalism. In 1853, she founded *The Provincial Freeman* with the purpose of giving a voice to the voiceless that was, according to the slogan, "Devoted to anti-slavery, temperance, and general literature" (Specia, 2018, p. 1). Notably, How (2022), echoing the opinion of Yee (1997), describes the paper as a strategy to make Mary Ann's voice heard. The paper was published weekly from March 24, 1853, and was aimed at Black Americans, especially enslaved people. As a journalist, Mary Ann would become part of "a long tradition of Black foreign journalists," including her contemporary Frederick Douglass and, later on W.E.B. DuBois. "Mostly operating within the realm of the Black press and writing for a Black audience," these journalists strove to bring "an often-overlooked Black perspective to world reporting" (Harris, 2023, p. 160).

The creation of *The Provincial Freeman* made Mary Ann one of Canada's first female journalists, and she was the first Black woman in Canada and North America to publish a newspaper. She wrote many of the articles in the paper herself and often traveled back to the United States to research and gather information for her publication. She would take great personal risks to bring her paper and its message across the border from Canada into America, riding a horse or taking a stagecoach to different communities. When there, she would discuss her life in Canada and collect subscriptions to pay for the paper. Mary Ann wrote diverse articles for the publication, including several on Canada West, the abolition of slavery, and the place of African Americans in American society. To this end, Mary Ann often used *The Provincial Freeman* to publicize the successes of Black persons living in freedom in Canada to promote emigration to the country. In reference to her self-made nature, the motto of the paper was "self-reliance is the true road to independence."

According to her biographer, Jane Rhodes, "It is clear that the impetus for starting a newspaper lay with Shadd, but she was careful to surround herself with male supporters" (Rhodes, 1999, p. 70). This strategy overcame the challenges posed by her female sex. For example, *The Provincial Freeman* was co-edited by Samuel Ringgold Ward, an escaped enslaved person and well-known public speaker living in Toronto, and the newspaper's named corresponding editor was Alexander McArthur, a White congregational minister. As newspapers and editorships were then considered to be a male occupation, Mary Ann was careful to ensure that the newspaper appeared to be run by men in order not to alienate her readership. To this end, she listed Ward as editor on the masthead of the paper and did not list her own name or take any credit for the articles that she wrote in order to conceal the fact that the newspaper was run and edited by a woman.

Over the course of its six-to-seven-year run, *The Provincial Freeman* was published from three locations: Windsor (1853–1854), Toronto (1854–1855), and Chatham (1855–1857). Following the publication of the first edition of the paper, Mary Ann spent a year collecting subscriptions for *The Provincial Freeman* and building interest for her publication by entering the lecture circuit. As a result of her efforts, the newspaper began publishing weekly out of Toronto on March 25, 1854.

The motto of the newspaper, "self-reliance is the true road to independence" echoed the importance Mary Ann placed upon Black self-sufficiency and integration into Canadian society. She advised readers of *The Provincial Freeman* to insist on fair treatment and resort to legal action if their rights were not respected. She also ensured that the newspaper actively championed women's rights and provided opportunities for other Black women to become published writers, showcase their accomplishments, and partake in benevolent activities.

Many others were also involved in the activities of Mary Ann's newspaper, including some of the core Black leaders of the day, such as H. Ford Douglas and Reverend William P. Newman, both of whom were involved as editors and contributors to the paper. Also, after the newspaper moved to Chatham, Canada West in 1855, Mary Ann's brother Isaac was appointed editor and her sister Amelia, and sister-in-law Amelia Freeman Shadd, contributed articles and served as temporary editors. The reason why the newspaper needed temporary editors was that Mary Ann often engaged in investigative reporting and muckraking (a form of exposé journalism) to attack institutions such as the Black church or those she believed were engaged in wrongdoing. Mary Ann also frequently traveled to go on speaking tours in Canada and the United States to financially support the paper, which was difficult as most of its readership was poor and uneducated, so it was dependent on a small, educated, elite group of readers for support.

However, the progressive, unorthodox approach adopted by *The Provincial Freeman* was criticized by some who might have been potential allies. This is because Mary Ann held many firm, entrenched, and sometimes controversial views. For example, she criticized abolitionists who did not fight for full equality and supported segregated communities and schools and who denounced refugee associations that raised funds to support fugitive slaves while allowing free Black people to live in poverty. One critic from a rival paper expressed unhappiness with her views when they wrote: "Miss Shadd has said and written many things which we think will add nothing to her credit as a lady" (Specia, 2018, p. 1). But Mary Ann did not care about being a lady; she wanted to have a voice. Consequently, she received a lot of criticism from Black male leaders and even from some Black women due to her visibility and how vocal she was. Also, Mary Ann defied the traditional expectation that a woman's place was in the home. She said: "I'm opening the door for you, for Black women, and I'm proud that I'm doing that and I'm trying to create a space for you to have a voice" (Specia, 2018, p. 1).

Mary Ann was a woman who practiced what she preached. Notably, her belief in education for all often came at her own expense. For example, Mary Ann placed a notice in *The Provincial Freeman* on June 18, 1859, for a school she and her sister ran in Chatham, advertising it as open to all, even those who could not pay:

> Mrs. A.F. Shadd, and Mrs. M.A.S. Cary's School is now open. Persons having children, and desiring that they shall have a practical English education, send in at once; as an education is the only sure means to secure success in any pursuit in life. No complectical distinction will be admitted in this school but all who desire instruction will be impartially dealt with irrespective of creed or color. The only object of the school is to benefit those desiring an education. Those unable to pay—and particularly the children of poor widows—will receive instruction free of charge. (How, 2022, p. 222)

This advertisement appears to encapsulate Mary Ann's principles, including her belief that everyone should have a right to an education and that there should be no social barriers between people of different races.

In 1856, Mary Ann married Virginia-born Toronto barber and businessman Thomas Fauntleroy Cary. They had two children, Sarah Elizabeth and Linton, but Thomas sadly died in 1860 whilst Mary Ann was pregnant with Linton, leaving her with two small children and three stepchildren.

Around that time, *The Provincial Freeman* finally succumbed to financial pressure and folded. There is some debate as to whether it continued publication until 1859 or 1860. The paper is thought to have been published until 1860 as an advertisement for it was put in other newspapers that year; however, no copies of *The Provincial Freeman* published in 1860 survive, with the last surviving issues bearing the dates of January and June 1859 respectively. Nevertheless, the paper's six-or-seven-year run meant that it survived longer than most mid-century Black newspapers, despite the challenges Mary Ann experienced in securing funding which led to some gaps in publishing. Having survived seven years and three places, the newspaper was among a small group of influential Black publications, including newspapers edited by the well-known African American abolitionist Frederick Douglass. Furthermore, the newspaper provided a vital voice for the Black community in Canada and also provided insights into their activities for modern-day researchers.

On the Fringe

After her newspaper finally folded, Mary Ann's advocacy work continued, and she taught at an integrated school in Chatham where she remained for the first few years of the American Civil War. Then, in 1863, having been hired by Dr. Martin Delany, Mary Ann began work as a recruiting officer for the Union Army in Indiana and also encouraged African Americans to join the fight on the Union side against slavery. She moved to Detroit in 1867 and earned a teaching certificate in 1868, which enabled her to teach in public schools. She also bought a house and became involved in local politics with other citizens campaigning for social reform. In 1869, she left Detroit for Washington, DC. There, she founded a school for the children of freed slaves to offer them more opportunities in life.

When she moved to Washington, DC, Mary Ann also enrolled in the first class of Howard University Law School in Washington, DC, attending evening classes at Howard and teaching children during the day. However, in 1871, Mary Ann withdrew from Howard University and later claimed that she had been refused a law degree due to her sex. Around this time, she also worked as a political activist and writer, writing for a local African American newspaper, *The New National Era,* and gave public speeches to encourage Black Americans to work together to recover from slavery.

In the 1870s, Mary Ann also became involved in the women's suffrage movement. She was a founding member of the Colored Women's Progressive Franchise Association and became a member of the National Woman Suffrage Association (NWSA) in 1881, having previously spoken at the latter's 1878 convention. Some of Mary Ann's other suffrage work involved advocating for the 14th and 15th Amendments at a hearing of the House Judiciary Committee in January 1874. The 14th Amendment defined citizenship while the 15th Amendment gave African American men the right to vote. Mary Ann spoke to support the 15th Amendment but still criticized it for failing to give women the right to vote also. She addressed the committee as part of a group of women petitioning for the right to vote, telling them that:

> I am not vain enough to suppose for a moment that words of mine could add one iota of weight to the arguments from these learned and earnest women... as a colored woman... [and yet as] a resident of this district, a taxpayer she only had a portion of rights of a male counterpart despite her equal contribution to society. (Specia, 2018, p. 1)

In fact, Mary Ann's affiliation with the NWSA came about partly in protest that the 15th Amendment had granted Black men but not Black women the vote. Also, in 1874, Mary Ann, along with 63 other women, tried to register to vote in a future Washington, DC election. Mary Ann was among a group of both Black and White women (including Susan B. Anthony) who adopted a strategy of attempting to register to vote and showing up at the polls as an act of civil disobedience in order to challenge women's citizenship status under the 14th Amendment.

Furthermore, in 1876, representing 94 Black women, she wrote to the NWSA asking for their names to be included on a statement demanding enfranchisement. Then, in 1880, she organized the all-Black Colored Women's Progressive Franchise Organization and, through that, campaigned for women's rights. While Mary Ann's suffrage work meant that she worked alongside key figures in the suffrage movement such as Susan B. Anthony and Elizabeth Cady Stanton, she was marginalized due to her status as a woman of color. For example, when she wrote to the NWSA in 1876 asking for the names of 94 Black women to be added to the franchise statement, the women were rebuffed. This rejection then led Mary Ann to form the Colored Women's Progressive Franchise Organization in 1880 to give her and other Black women a voice in the suffrage campaign. However, it would be many years before women gained the right to vote.

Lady Lawyer's Legacy

In 1881, Mary Ann returned to Howard University and in May 1883, she finally received her law degree at the age of 60, being one of the first Black women to do so. Although she was never admitted to the bar, "M.A. Shadd Cary, Esq., a colored lady lawyer" went on to proudly practice law for the rest of her life.

Mary Ann's final home was a brick row house on W Street in Northwest Washington, DC. At present, this house is a National Historic Landmark that helps visitors understand her life and work as an advocate for equal rights. Her last years were quiet and tragic. In 1892, her son Linton Cary tragically passed away at his sister's home, four days before Christmas. This was Mary Ann's final heartbreak. Linton was described by a local newspaper as "the support of his aged mother and sister" (Rhodes, 1999, p. 211).

Mary Ann died of stomach cancer on June 5, 1893, at the home of her daughter Sarah, leaving an estate of $150. Her funeral was held at Israel Metropolitan African Methodist Episcopal Church, one of the oldest Black churches and home to Bethel Library and Historical Association, where she had given many public lectures. Mary Ann was buried at Columbia Harmony Cemetery in Washington, DC. However, the cemetery she was buried in was relocated to Maryland's National Harmony

Memorial Park in 1960 without gravestones, which means that her final resting place goes unmarked.

She died without a will and few worldly goods. When her daughter Sarah was appointed administrator of her mother's estate, its total value came to just $150. Mary Ann's most valued possessions were her books, including a collection of legal texts. This suggests that she valued her advocacy work far more than material possessions.

Perhaps one of the best descriptions of Mary Ann's work comes from the sociologist, historian, and civil rights activist W.E.B. DuBois. Writing in the 1920s, in an essay entitled "The Damnation of Women," he described Mary Ann in the following terms:

> Well-educated, vivacious, with determination shining from her sharp eyes, she threw herself single-handed into the great Canadian pilgrimage when thousands of hunted Black men hurried northward and crept beneath the protection of the lion's paw. (Specia, 2018, p. 1)

Mary Ann also inspired praise from her contemporary, Frederick Douglass, who primarily stressed her journalistic achievements when he wrote about her work in a paper entitled "Canada" dated July 4, 1856: "She displayed industry, financial capacity, and literary ability of a high order... She is a pioneer among colored women, and every colored lady in the country has a right to feel proud of her" (Streitmatter, 1994, p. 36). Mary Ann was thus admired by the Black community both in her own lifetime and afterwards.

Mary Ann is still commemorated and remembered today. In 1994, she was designated as a person of National Historic Significance in Canada and the Mary Shadd Public School, named in her honor, opened in Scarborough, Ontario in 1985. Her last home in Washington, DC bears a historic plaque, as do both the Toronto addresses from which *The Provincial Freeman* was published, and as do the newspaper's headquarters in Chatham-Kent County, Ontario. Most recently, on October 9, 2020, Mary Ann was featured in a Google Doodle on the occasion of her 197th birthday and, in 2021, a post office in her birthplace, Wilmington, Delaware was named after her.

Despite all the barriers she broke, Mary Ann has not been much remembered. Thankfully, this injustice is being righted as her work has received more attention and acclaim in recent years.

Chapter Six
Conclusion
Uniting Voices

The collective impact of the lives and works of Harriet Tubman, Sarah Grimké, Angelina Grimké Weld, Sojourner Truth, Elizabeth Heyrick, and Mary Ann Cary Tubman was considerable. All six women raised their voices to speak up "while female" for the abolitionist movement, as well as the women's rights and suffrage movements in the 19th century and beyond, and other social causes of the day. Below, we will look at connections between them all and the impact of their combined legacy.

Common Themes

All six women were campaigners against slavery. Harriet, Sarah, Angelina, Sojourner, and Elizabeth as active abolitionists and Mary Ann as an advocate of Canada as a new home for those escaping slavery and the consequences of the Fugitive Slave Act. Apart from this, there are other interesting connections between these women. First, both Harriet and Truth escaped slavery—Harriet via the Underground Railroad and Truth by simply walking out of her master's house with her baby. Also, both Harriet and Mary Ann were involved with the activities of the Underground Railroad. Harriet was actively involved as a guide, helping numerous enslaved people find their way to freedom while Mary Ann's parents sheltered many enslaved people traveling to freedom via the Underground Railroad.

Those women who were not enslaved campaigned against slavery from a position of privilege. The Grimké sisters had grown up in South Carolina in a slave-owning family while Elizabeth was a British woman from a comfortable, middle-class background, although her Unitarian family were social campaigners who also opposed slavery. Mary Ann was also privileged for a Black woman of the period and had access to an education in a way that many of her peers did not. But despite their access to privilege, all four of these women had the capacity to sympathize with and advocate for those less fortunate than themselves.

Many of the women we have surveyed were actively involved in the women's rights movement and the campaign for women's suffrage. The Grimké sisters, Mary Ann, and Truth all vocally campaigned for women's suffrage. Inspired by resistance to their public-speaking efforts on the grounds that they were women, from the 1830s onwards, the Grimké sisters promoted women's rights and supported women's suffrage. Meanwhile, Truth became acquainted with the women's rights movement in the 1840s, around the same time she first encountered abolitionism.

Her feminism is an example of intersectionality in the sense that Truth was multiply disadvantaged due to her race, her status as enslaved, and as a woman. These experiences led her to campaign on the behalf of both women and the enslaved, often referencing women's rights in her speeches. Then, after the Civil War, Truth's focus became women's suffrage. Like Truth, Mary Ann also focused much of her advocacy work on women's suffrage after the Civil War. She was involved with the NWSA and formed the Colored Women's Progressive Franchise Association in 1880.

Although Harriet is often said to have been heavily involved in the women's rights movement, her role in such activities appears to have been exaggerated. She did agree with the proposition that women should have the vote, but she never actively assisted the suffragists or the women's suffrage movement.

Meanwhile, Elizabeth also advocated for women having a role in public life and social movements, motivating other women to spearhead the campaign to boycott sugar produced in the West Indies, as this product was made using slave labor, and playing an integral role in the formation of women-only anti-slavery groups. Elizabeth also played a central role in the formation of the Female Society for Birmingham in 1825. That group then influenced the formation of women's anti-slavery groups in the United Kingdom and the United States. By 1831, there were 73 such organizations that had been formed in the United

Kingdom.

Harriet, Elizabeth, and Mary Ann all also campaigned for other political causes outside of slavery. Harriet advocated women's rights, helped the poor, and set up schools for freed slaves. Her last act of philanthropy was setting up a care home for elderly Black people that opened in 1908. From the 1790s onwards, Elizabeth was actively involved in the promotion of many social causes, from the banning of bull-baiting to labor rights to the plight of migrant workers. Meanwhile, Mary Ann actively promoted the right for everyone to access education, regardless of their race or financial status. She also campaigned for the end of social segregation, believing that Black and White people should socialize freely with one another without constraints.

Both Elizabeth and Mary Ann either lived or spent considerable portions of their lives outside of the United States. Elizabeth lived in Britain, while Mary Ann spent over a decade living in Canada. Harriet also spent a few years in Canada. Their examples show how slavery was not just a problem for the United States; it also impacted on other parts of the world including Europe and the Caribbean.

Collective Influence on the Abolition Movement and Societal Perceptions

One of the key themes in the collective stories of all six women is that all faced resistance from male peers due to their gender. While male abolitionists agreed that slavery needed to be abolished, they did not always agree that women should play a public role in promoting its abolition. For this reason, Elizabeth encountered resistance from her male peers when she promoted an immediate rather than gradual approach to the abolition of slavery, and the Grimké sisters were resented for having the audacity to speak in public in favor of abolitionism. Truth also encountered a mixed response from her abolitionist peers, such as Frederick Douglass, who found her speech simple and lacking in gravitas. Furthermore, Mary Ann fell out with many of her male peers such as Henry Bibb, who also promoted emigration to Canada as a way to escape slavery. This is because they disapproved of her forthright views on issues such as segregation.

The prejudices and injustices that these women encountered due to their gender made them even more determined to succeed. Most of them spoke up in favor of women's rights and women's suffrage. The resistance they encountered from their male peers in the abolitionist movement usually led to a natural progression to work to promote women's rights.

Lasting Legacies

The end of slavery in the United States in 1865 did not mean the beginning of equality for formerly enslaved people. Instead, many Black people, especially those living in the South, continued to experience segregation and marginalization. Consequently, the fight for equal rights continued throughout the 19th century and well into the 20th century. One of the eventual legacies of the fight for abolition was thus the Civil Rights Movement that campaigned for the end of segregation and equal rights in the United States. This movement finally made the necessary gains in the 1960s but not without considerable sacrifices in the meantime.

Despite their contributions to the women's suffrage movement, none of our six women lived to see women gain the vote. It was not until June 4, 1919, that Congress passed the 19th Amendment, which granted all women in the United States the right to vote, although some individual states such as Wyoming, Colorado, and Michigan had granted women the right to vote before that date. Meanwhile, British women gained the right to vote between 1918 and 1928, while in Canada the right to vote was sporadically given according to the territory, with women in Quebec not gaining the vote until 1949.

The work of Harriet, Sarah, Angelina, Truth, Elizabeth, and Mary Ann continues to inspire and influence people today. Their stories are a reminder of the power of both individual and collective action. The struggle for equality and civil rights continues today. Women's voices are still being silenced, even within movements for social justice. Events such as the death of George Floyd in 2020 that resulted from police brutality and sparked worldwide protest demonstrate how the struggle for equality and civil rights continues today.

Courage, Resistance, and Determination

All six women displayed courage, resistance, and determination in their extraordinary lives. Both Harriet and Truth escaped slavery, an act that must have taken considerable courage given that the consequences would have been severe if they had been caught. Mary Ann and her family were also courageous as they chose to be involved with the Underground Railroad by sheltering escaping slaves, as this act could have had serious repercussions for them. Furthermore, Sarah and Angelina chose to step out of the accepted role of women by becoming public speakers at a time when women were discouraged from doing so Elizabeth showed courage for going against the voices and opinions of male abolitionists when she called for "immediate, not gradual abolition."

Another indication of the resilience and determination of this group of six extraordinary women is that all apart from Angelina spent most of their lives as single women. Indeed, Angelina was single at the height of her public speaking career and only seems to have given it up on the

CONCLUSION

advice of her husband. As for the others, Sarah remained single her entire life, while Harriet's first marriage was short lived, and she only found happiness with her second husband in later life. Truth's marriage fell apart quickly while Mary Ann was widowed after four years of marriage and Elizabeth after eight. It is remarkable at a time when women were expected to be married or under control of a father or brother that all these women were able to lead such independent lives without needing to rely on a man for support.

It is also notable that all of the women studied in this book broke free of the chains of societal expectations. Sarah and Angelina Grimké moved away from their family in South Carolina and devoted themselves to the abolitionist movement and later to women's suffrage despite having come from a slave-holding family, while Elizabeth dedicated her widowhood to her career as a social reformer when she could have lived quietly with her family or remarried. Mary Ann always worked as a teacher, journalist, and abolitionist and did not let marriage or motherhood stop her from pursuing her ambitions. Meanwhile, Harriet spent her life helping other enslaved people escape via the Underground Railroad and later dedicated her life to aiding the Unionist side in the Civil War and promoting other social causes. Truth also forged an independent life for herself as a preacher and, later, as an abolitionist and women's rights campaigner.

Summary

The lives of each of the six women covered here is important as these lives demonstrate the meaning of having a voice. Although two out of the six were born into slavery and all were disadvantaged due to their gender in the times in which they lived, all these women had the courage to defy the status quo and speak out for what they believed in. By collectively having a voice, these women were able to contribute to eventually successfully putting an end to the unjust institution of slavery and to paving the path toward women's suffrage. However, many women remain silenced today as their circumstances and societal pressure mean they are unable to speak up for themselves or their rights. The examples of Harriet, Sarah, Angelina, Truth, Elizabeth, and Mary Ann thus give us hope that no woman might be silenced because of her gender in future.

The most vulnerable members of society in the 18th and 19th centuries, such as the young, poor, immigrant, uneducated, female and Black, were ruthlessly exploited and silenced by the most powerful, such as male captains of industry, politicians, journalists, and church leaders. Many may argue that they still are. Yet our women were not passive victims. They were the first to band together, take direct action, and speak up for their rights.

The memorable and inspirational accounts of the lives of all six women tell the reader all about the experience of women in the 18th and 19th centuries and how each of these individual women defied the expectations society set of her. They also draw on how the abolitionist cause liberated these women and gave them a voice. Thus, by involving themselves in the abolitionist cause, these women both liberated the enslaved and gave themselves and other women a voice. For this reason, Harriet, Sarah, Angelina, Truth, Elizabeth, and Mary Ann remain inspirational today and deserve to be remembered.

If you have enjoyed reading ***Voices of Freedom***, it would be greatly appreciated if you would be so kind as to leave a review on Amazon. Credit is due to you as a reader for having the curiosity to want to explore this subject and help restore the stories of women who have often been left behind and forgotten by, or written out of, history. Reviews make all the difference to independently published authors. Thank you!

About the Author

Elise Baker has a lifelong interest in women's history and feminism. Her passion is excavating the past to unearth the stories of women whose remarkable feats and accomplishments have been buried and forgotten because of their gender in the hope that they can fuel and inspire women of today to face adversity and discrimination with courage. In learning about the achievements of these remarkable women, we address the serious shortage of women in documented history. There are countless women leaders whose contributions have been forgotten. Often they put their lives on the line, knowing that their efforts would likely go unrecognized. Their stories offer a more balanced perspective on history. May they serve as inspiration to women to continue to make a difference and occupy important spaces.

Elise's maternal family, from the borderlands of the Czech Republic, became refugees with no country to belong to after the Second World War and dispersed all over the world. She grew up listening to her grandmother's recollections of this time, and believes that understanding and learning from the bravery of ordinary women is essential in shaping the future. She holds an Honors degree and a Postgraduate Diploma that led to a career as a librarian, archivist, and eventually an editor for television. She loves traveling to different countries and experiencing different cultures. When she's not reading or writing, she enjoys walking with her dog along the beach and seeing plays at the theater with family and friends.

To see more books in the *Brave Women in History* and *Brave Women Who Changed the Course of WWII* series, please visit www.elise-baker.com

Also By

To keep an eye out for new titles, bringing more forgotten stories of women's achievements to light,
and to sign up for Elise Baker's monthly newsletter **Brave Women in History** please visit: www.elise-baker.com

Blazing the Way: *Match Girls, Mill Girls and Other Fiery Females Whose Strikes Sparked a Revolution in Women's Rights*

Women Code Breakers: The Best Kept Secret of WWII *True Stories of Female Code Breakers Whose Top-Secret Work Helped Win World War II*

ALSO BY

Princess, Countess, Socialite, Spy: *True Stories of High-Society Ladies Turned WWII Spies*

Women Rescuers of WWII: *True Stories of Unsung Women Heroes Who Rescued Refugees and Allied Servicemen in WWII*

Nightingales, Bluebirds and Angels of Mercy: *True Stories of the Courage and Heroism of Nurses on the Front Line in WWII*

References & Bibliography

Anastas, K., (2023). *Timeline and map of women's suffrage legislation state by state 1838–1919.* University of Washington Mapping American Social Movements Project. https://depts.washington.edu/moves/WomanSuffrage_map.shtml

Andrews, W.L. (Ed.). (2003). *Classic African American women's narratives.* Oxford University Press.

Astin, H.S., & Leland, C. (1991). *Women of influence, women of vision: A cross-generational study of leaders and social change.* John Wiley & Sons.

Bates, P., & Patel, A. (2023). *Building a culture of inclusivity: Effective internal communication for diversity, equality, and inclusion.* Kogan Page.

Bennett, M. (2005). *Democratic discourses: The radical abolition movement and antebellum American literature.* Rutgers University Press.

Benowitz, J.M. (2017). Truth, Sojourner (ca. 1797–1883). *Encyclopedia of American women and religion (2nd ed.).* ABC-CLIO.

Biography.com Editors. (2021). *Mary Ann Shadd Cary.* Biography.com. https://www.biography.com/activists

/mary-ann-shadd-cary

Birney, C.H. (2004). *The Grimké sisters*. Kessinger Publishing LLC.

Black Women's Suffrage. (2023). *Sojourner Truth, c.1797–1893*. https://blackwomenssuffrage.dp.la/key-figures/sojournerTruth

Bownas, J.L. (2020). *Slavery, freedom, and conflict: A story of two Birminghams*. Sussex Academic Press.

Boyer, P.S. (2023). *The enduring vision: A history of the American people (10th ed.)*. Wadsworth Publishing Co., Inc.

Bradford, S.H. (1869). *Scenes in the life of Harriet Tubman*. W.J. Moses.

Bradford, S. (1993). *Harriet Tubman: the Moses of her people*. Applewood.

The Editors of Encyclopaedia Britannica. (2023). *Industrial revolution causes and effects*. Encyclopedia Britannica. https://www.britannica.com/summary/Industrial-Revolution-Causes-and-Effects

British Library. (2023a). *The slave trade–A historical background*. https://www.bl.uk/learning/histcitizen/campaignforabolition/abolitionbackground/abolitionintro.html

British Library. (2023b). *"Immediate, not gradual abolition" by Elizabeth Heyrick*. https://www.bl.uk/collection-items/immediate-not-gradual-abolition

British Library. (2023c). *Source 9: Elizabeth Heyrick*. https://www.bl.uk/learning/histcitizen/campaignforabolition/sources/antislavery/sugarboycott/sugboycott.html

Cervenak, S.J. (2012). Gender, class, and the performance of a black (anti) enlightenment–resistances of David Walker and Sojourner Truth. *Palimpsest: A Journal on Women, Gender, and the Black International, 1* (1): 68–86.

Chidi, S.L. (2014). *The greatest Black achievers in history*. Lulu.com.

Clark, C. (1995). *The communitarian movement: The radical challenge of the Northampton Association*. Cornell University Press.

Clinton, C. (2004). *Harriet Tubman: The road to freedom*. Little, Brown and Company.

Coates, S. (2010). *Abraham Lincoln and Sojourner Truth*. The New York Times. https://archive.nytimes.com/artsbeat.blogs.nytimes.com/2010/10/29/abraham-lincoln-and-sojourner-truth/

Cross, L.D. (2010). *The Underground Railroad: The long journey to freedom in Canada*. James Lorimer Limited.

Cullen-DuPont, K. (2000). *Encyclopedia of women's history in America. (2nd ed.)*. Facts On File, Inc.

Cunningham, R. (2016). Review: African Canadians in union blue: Volunteering for the cause in the civil war by Richard M. Reid. *Army History*, 40–41.

Davidson, B. (1961). *The African slave* trade. James Currey.

DeHart, V. (2020). *Elizabeth Heyrick, mother of immediatism.*

The Women's Print History Project.

https://womensprinthistoryproject.com/blog/post/27

Dionne, E. (2020). *Lifting as we climb: Black women's battle for the ballot box.* Viking.

Dunbar, E.A. (2019). *She came to slay: The life and times of Harriet Tubman.* Simon & Schuster.

Durso, P.R. (2003). *The power of women: The life and writings of Sarah Moore Grimké.* Mercer University Press.

Editorial Team. (2019). *Elizabeth Heyrick: Abolitionist campaigner.* Black History Month.

https://www.blackhistorymonth.org.uk/article/section/history-of-slavery/4321/

Eisenstadt, P. (Ed.). (2005). *The encyclopedia of New York State.* Syracuse University Press.

Eltis, D., & Richardson, D. (2002). The numbers game. In D. Northrup (Ed.). *The Atlantic slave trade (2nd ed.).* Houghton Mifflin Co.

Este, D. (2018). African Canadians: "Still in search of the promised land." In S. Guo, & L. Wong (Eds.). *Immigration, racial, and ethnic studies in 150 years of Canada: Retrospects and prospects.* Brill.

Fadeland, B.L. (1971). Grimké. In E.T. James (Ed.). *Notable American women: A biographical dictionary (Vol. 1 A–F).* The Belknap Press of Harvard University.

Faust, D.G. (2022). *The Grimké sisters and the indelible stain of slavery*. The Atlantic. https://www.theatlantic.com/magazine/archive/2022/12/the-Grimkés-legacy-of-slavery-book-review/671901/

Feagin, J.R., Vera, H., & Imani, N. (1996). *The agony of education: Black students at white colleges and universities*. Routledge.

Ferguson, M. (Ed.). (1998). *Nine black women: An anthology of nineteenth-century writers from the United States, Canada, Bermuda, and the Caribbean*. Routledge.

Ferris, J.C. (2003). *Demanding justice: A story about Mary Ann Shadd Cary*. Carolrhoda Books, Inc.

Fitch, S.P., & Mandziuk, R. (1997). *Sojourner Truth as orator: Wit, story, and song*. Greenwood.

Floyd, J. (2022). *US Treasury confirms Harriet Tubman $20 bill is coming–but here's why you'll have to wait*. The Grio. https://thegrio.com/2022/02/13/us-treasury-harriet-tubman-20-bill/

Fortney, A. (2016). *The Fortney encyclical of Black history: The world's true Black history. (1st ed.)*. Xlibris.

Gigsby, D.G. (2015). *Enduring truths: Sojourner's shadows and substance*. University of Chicago Press.

Gilbert, O. (1998). *Narrative of Sojourner Truth*. Penguin.

Gordon-Reed, A. (2021). *Black America's neglected origin stories*. The Atlantic. https://www.theatlantic.com/magazine/archive/2021/06/estebanico-first-africans-america/618714/

The Grimké Sisters Tour. (2023). *The Grimké sisters tour*. https://Grimkésisterstour.com/

Grozier, G. (2022). *Stories from Mount Hope: The amazing Grimké sisters*. City of Boston. https://www.boston.gov/news/stories-mount-hope-amazing-Grimké-sisters

Grundy, I. (2004). *Elizabeth Heyrick. In Oxford Dictionary of National Biography*. Oxford University Press.

Grundy, I. (2010). *Elizabeth Heyrick (1869–1831)*. Women's History Network. https://womenshistorynetwork.org/black-history-month-elizabeth-heyrick-1869-1831/

Hague, W. (2008). *William Wilberforce: The life of the great anti-slave trade campaigner*. Harper Perennial.

Hamilton, N.A. (2002a). *American social leaders & activists*. Facts On File, Inc.

Hamilton, N.A. (2002b). *Renegades: A chronology of social and political dissent in the United States*. Routledge.

Hans, S. (2019). *"Harriet" review–Thrilling drama about the abolitionist Harriet Tubman*. The Observer. https://www.theguardian.com/film/2019/nov/24/harriet-review-harriet-tubman-biopic-cynthia-erivo-janelle-monae

Harmer, H. (2001). *The Longman's companion to slavery, emancipation, and civil rights*. Routledge.

Harriet Tubman Underground Railroad Byway. (2023). *About Harriet Tubman*. https://harriettubmanbyway.org/harriet-tubman/

Harris, H.R. (2015). Freedman's bureau records of 4 million former slaves to be released Friday. *Washington Post*.
https://www.washingtonpost.com/news/local/wp/2015/06/19/freedmens-bureau-records-of-4-million-former-slaves-released-today/

Harris, G.A. (2023). *Social justice and liberation struggles: The photojournalistic and public relations career of Alexander McAllister Rivera JR*. Lexington Books.

Hartweave, S. (2022). *Heyrick, Elizabeth (1769–1831)*. In C. Goucher (Ed.) Women who changed the world: Their lives, challenges, and accomplishments throughout history. ABC--CLIO.

Hernandez-Wilson, J. (2011). *The 7 secrets of women who have their cake and eat it too! "Creating the life of your dreams by building self-confidence."* Xlibris Corporation.

Heyrick, E. (1824). *Immediate, not gradual abolition; or, an inquiry into the shortest, safest, and most effectual means of getting rid of West Indian slavery (1st ed.)*. Richard Clay.

Historic England. (2015). *Unsung heroines of the anti-slavery movement remembered*.
https://historicengland.org.uk/whats-new/news/anti-slavery-heroines/

History.com Editors. (2023a). *Industrial revolution*. History.com.
https://www.history.com/topics/industrial-revolution

/industrial-revolution

History.com Editors. (2023b). *Harriet Tubman*. History.com. https://www.history.com/topics/black-history/harriet-tubman

History.com Editors. (2023c). *Sojourner Truth*. History.com. https://www.history.com/topics/black-history/sojourner-truth

Hochschild, A. (2005). *Bury the chains: The British struggle to abolish slavery*. Pan Books.

Holcomb, J.L. (2016). *Moral commerce: Quakers and the transatlantic boycott of the slave labor economy*. Cornell University Press.

Horn, G.M. (2010). *Sojourner Truth: Speaking up for freedom*. Crabtree Publishing Company.

Hornsby, A. (2011). *Black America: A state-by-state historical encyclopedia (Vol. 1: A–M)*. Greenwood.

Horton, J.O., & Horton, L.E. (2005). *Slavery and the making of America*. Oxford University Press.

How, S. (2022). Cary, Mary Ann Shadd (1823–1893). In C. Goucher (Ed.). *Women who changed the world: Their lives, challenges, and accomplishments throughout history*. ABC-CLIO.

Hughes, K. (2014). Gender roles in the 19th century. *The British Library*. https://www.bl.uk/romantics-and-victorians/articles/gender-roles-in-the-19th-century

Humez, J. (2003). *Harriet Tubman: The life and life sto-

ries. University of Wisconsin Press.

The Independent. (2022). *Documents rediscovered: Sojourner Truth's fight to save son*.
https://www.independent.co.uk/news/peter-ap-new-york-dna-alabama-b2100836.html

James, F., & Shuttleworth, R. (2017). *Susanna Watts and Elizabeth Heyrick: Collaborative campaigning in the Midlands, 1820–34*. In A.O. Winckles, & A. Rehbein (Eds.). Women's literary networks and romanticism: "A tribe of authoresses." Liverpool University Press.

Johnson, P.E., & Wilentz, S. (1994). *The kingdom of Matthias: A story of sex and salvation in 19th-century America*. Oxford University Press.

Joy, M.S. (2011). *Abolitionist movement. Immigration to United States*. https://immigrationtounitedstates.org/323-abolitionist-movement.html

Kidd, S.M. (2014). *The invention of wings*. Penguin.

Kirby, J. (2016). *Historians and the Church of England: Religion and historical scholarship, 1870–1920*. Oxford University Press.

Knight, L.W. (2018). *Voices in time: Epistolary activism*. Lapham's Quarterly.
https://www.laphamsquarterly.org/roundtable/voices-time-Grimké

Knight, L.W. (2023). *About the Grimké sisters*. Louise W. Knight: Author and Historian.
https://www.louisewknight.com/about-the-Grimké-si

sters.html

Krass, P., & Wagner, H.L. (2005). *Sojourner Truth: Antislavery activist*. Chelsea House.

Lamb, G.M. (2005). *The peculiar color of racial justice*. The Christian Science Monitor. https://www.csmonitor.com/2005/0125/p15s01-bogn.html

Lantier, P. (2010). *Harriet Tubman: Conductor on the Underground Railroad*. Crabtree Publishing Company.

Larson, K.C. (2004). *Bound for the promised land: Harriet Tubman, portrait of an American hero*. Ballantine Books.

Larson, K.C. (2022). *Harriet Tubman: A reference guide to her life and works*. Rowman & Littlefield.

Lerner, G. (1998). *The Grimké sisters from South Carolina: Pioneers for women's rights and abolition*. Oxford University Press.

Library of Congress. (1998). *Sojourner Truth*. https://www.loc.gov/exhibits/odyssey/educate/truth.html

Library of Congress. (2023a). *Immigration to the United States, 1851–1900*. https://www.loc.gov/classroom-materials/united-states-history-primary-source-timeline/rise-of-industrial-america-1876-1900/immigration-to-united-states-1851-1900/

Library of Congress, (2023b*). John Bull and Uncle Sam: Four centuries of British-American relations:*

From abolition to equal rights.
https://www.loc.gov/exhibits/british/brit-4.html

Lusane, C. (2022). *Twenty dollars and change: Harriet Tubman and the ongoing fight for racial justice and democracy.* City Light Books.

Mabee, C. (1993). *Sojourner Truth: Slave, prophet, legend.* New York University Press.

Malaspina, A. (2009). *Harriet Tubman.* Chelsea House.

Maloof, T. (2017). *Harriet Tubman: Leading others to liberty.* Teacher Created Materials.

Marshall, K.J. (2019). *History of painting.* Simon & Schuster.

McCone, B. (2021). *Elizabeth Heyrick's consumer campaign to abolish slavery.* Grassroots Economic Organizing. https://geo.coop/articles/elizabeth-heyricks-consumer-campaign-abolish-slavery

Melder, K.E. (1997). *Beginnings of sisterhood: The American woman's rights movement, 1800–1850.* Schocken Books.

Melish, J.P. (2016). *Disowning slavery: Gradual emancipation and "race" in New England, 1780–1860.* Cornell University Press.

Michael, P.H. (2008). *Guide to freedom: Rediscovering the Underground Railroad in one United States county.* Underground Railroad Free Press Books.

Michals, D. (2015). *Angelina Grimké Weld (1805–1879).* National Women's History Museum.
https://www.womenshistory.org/education-resources/

biographies/angelina-Grimké-weld

Middleton, D.J. (2021). *45 people, places, & events in black history you should know*. Unique Coloring.

Midgley, C. (1995). *Women against slavery*: The British campaigners, 1780–1870. Routledge.

Midgley, C. (2011). The dissenting voice of Elizabeth Heyrick: An exploration of the links between gender, religious dissent, and anti-slavery radicalism. In E.J . Clapp, & J.R. Jeffrey (Eds.). *Women, dissent, and anti-slavery in Britain and America, 1790–1865*. Oxford University Press.

Miller, J.A. (2021). *Guest kickass women in history: Elizabeth Heyrick*. Smart Bitches, Trashy Books. https://smartbitchestrashybooks.com/2021/06/guest-kickass-women-in-history-elizabeth-heyrick/

Milmo, C. (2015). *Slavery: How women's key role in abolition has yet to receive the attention it deserves.* The Independent. https://www.independent.co.uk/news/uk/home-news/slavery-how-women-s-key-role-in-abolition-has-yet-to-receive-the-attention-it-deserves-10467431.html

Murphy, L.G. (2011). *Sojourner Truth: A biography*. Greenwood.

Murrill, B. (2021). *The Grimké sisters*. Kyria. https://kyrianetwork.com/the-Grimké-sisters/

National Archives. (2022). *19th amendment to the U.S. Constitution: Women's right to vote (1920)*. Archives.gov. https://www.archives.gov/milestone-documents/1

9th-amendment

National Archives. (2023). *13th amendment to the U.S. Constitution: Abolition of slavery (1865)*. Archives.gov https://www.archives.gov/milestone-documents/13th-amendment

National Park Service. (2015). *Grimké sisters*. https://www.nps.gov/wori/learn/historyculture/Grimké-sisters.htm

National Park Service. (2023a). *Sojourner Truth: Ain't I a woman?* https://www.nps.gov/articles/sojourner-truth.htm

National Park Service. (2023b). *Mary Ann Shadd Cary*. https://www.nps.gov/people/mary-ann-shadd-cary.htm

National Women's Hall of Fame. (2023). *Mary Ann Shadd Cary*. https://www.womenofthehall.org/inductee/mary-ann-shadd-cary/

Nies, J. (1977). *Nine women: Portraits from the American radical tradition*. University of California Press.

Niver, H.M. (2016). *Heroes of Black history: Sojourner Truth*. Gareth Stevens Publishing.

Norton, M.B., Kamensky, J., Sheriff, C., Blight, D.W., Chudacoff, H.P., Logevall, F., Bailey, B., & Michals, D. (2015). *A people & a nation: A history of the United States (10th ed.)*. Cengage Learning.

O'Dea Schenken, S. (1999). *From suffrage to the Senate: An encyclopedia of American women in politics (Vol. 1: a–m)*. ABC-CLIO.

Oertel, K.T. (2016). *Harriet Tubman: Slavery, the civil war, and civil rights in nineteenth-century America*. Routledge.

Owens, D.B.C. (2010). Cary, Mary Ann Shadd. In L. M. Alexander, & W.C. Ruker (Eds.). *Encyclopedia of African American History*. ABC-CLIO.

Painter, N.I. (1996). *Sojourner Truth: A life, a symbol*. Norton.

Perry, M.E. (2002). *Lift up thy voice: The Grimké family's journey from slaveholders to civil rights leaders*. Viking Penguin.

Portnony, A. (2005). *Their right to speak: Women's activism in the Indian and slave debates*. Harvard University Press.

Ramon, V.C. (2021). *Benjamin Drew: The refugee narratives of fugitive slaves in Canada*. Universitat de Valencia.

Rappaport, H. (2001). *Encyclopedia of women's social reformers (Vol. 1)*. ABC-CLIO.

Recchiuti, J.L. (2023). *Life after slavery for African Americans*. Khan Academy. https://www.khanacademy.org/humanities/us-history/civil-war-era/reconstruction/a/life-after-slavery

Reddie, R.S. (2007). *Abolition! The struggle to abolish slavery in the British colonies*. Lion Books.

Rhodes, J. (1999*). Mary Ann Shadd Cary: The black press and protest in the nineteenth century*. Indiana University Press.

Robertson, C.K. (2011). *A dangerous dozen: 12 Christians who threatened the status quo but taught us to live like Jesus*. SkyLight Path Publishing.

Rodriguez, J. (Ed.). (2007). *Encyclopedia of emancipation and abolition in the transatlantic world: vol. 1–3*. Routledge.

Ross, C. (2006). *Separate spheres or shared dominions? Shaping of Christian Theology in Context, 23*(4): 228–235.

Rugemer, E.B. (2018). *Slave law and politics of resistance in the early Atlantic world*. Harvard University Press.

Ruffin, F.E. (2002). *Sojourner Truth: Early abolitionist*. The Rosen Publishing Group, Inc.

Rummel, J. (2003). *African-American social leaders and activists*. Facts On File, Inc.

Rycenga, J. (2005). A great awakening: Women's intellect as a factor in early abolitionist movements, 1824–1834. *Journal of Feminist Studies in Religion, 21*(2): 31–59.

Rycenga, J. (2007). Heyrick, Elizabeth Coltman (1769–1831). In P. Hinks, & J.R. McKivigan (Eds.). *Encyclopedia of antislavery and abolition: Vol 1. a–i*. Greenwood Press.

Schultz, J.D., & Van Assendelft, L. (1999). *Encyclopedia of women in American politics*. Greenwood.

Sernett, M.C. (2007). *Harriet Tubman: Myth, memory, and history*. Duke University Press.

Sethi, A. (2014). *The invention of wings by Sue Monk Kidd–Review*. The Observer.

https://www.theguardian.com/books/2014/jan/05/invention-wings-monk-kidd-review

Shadd, A. (2023). *Mary Ann Shadd*. The Canadian Encyclopedia. https://www.thecanadianencyclopedia.ca/en/article/mary-ann-shadd

Simkin, J. (1997). *Elizabeth Heyrick*. Spartacus Educational. https://spartacus-educational.com/REheyrick.htm

Sklar, K.K. (2000). *Women's rights energies within the antislavery movement, 1830–1870: A brief history with documents*. Bedford/St. Martins.

Smith, D.E. (2007). Harriet Tubman (c. 1821–1913). In J.P. Rodriguez (Ed.). *Slavery in the United States: A social, political, and historical encyclopedia, Vol. 1*. ABC-CLIO.

Snodgrass, M.E. (2015). *The civil war era and reconstruction: An encyclopedia of social, political, cultural, and economic history*. Routledge.

The Sojourner Truth Project. (2023). *The Sojourner Truth project*. https://www.thesojournertruthproject.com/

Specia, M. (2018). Overlooked no more: How Mary Ann Shadd Cary shook up the abolitionist movement. *The New York Times*. https://www.nytimes.com/2018/06/06/obituaries/mary-ann-shadd-cary-abolitionist-overlooked.html

Stetson, E., & David, L. (1994). *Glorying in tribulation: The lifework of Sojourner Truth*. MSU Press.

Story of Leicester. (2023). *City stories: Elizabeth Heyrick*

& Susannah Watts. https://www.storyofleicester.info/city-stories/elizabeth-heyrick-susannah-watts/

Streitmatter, R. (1994). *Raising her voice: African-American women journalists who changed history*. The University Press of Kentucky.

Theerman, V. (2023). *The Grimké sisters: The Heyward-Washington House, abolition, & image creation*. The Charleston Museum. https://www.charlestonmuseum.org/news-events/the-Grimké-sisters/

This Far by Faith. (2023). *Sojourner Truth*. https://www.pbs.org/thisfarbyfaith/people/sojourner_truth.html

Tinubu, S., (2018). *Elizabeth Heyrick and the Birmingham ladies' society for the relief of negro slaves*. Birmingham Blogs. https://blog.bham.ac.uk/legalherstory/2018/03/15/elizabeth-heyrick-and-the-birmingham-ladies-society-for-the-relief-of-negro-slaves/

Tomkins, S. (2007). *William Wilberforce: A biography*. Lion Hudson.

Turley, D. (2011). Complicating the story: Religion and gender in historical writing on British and American anti-slavery. In E.J. Clapp & J.R Jeffrey (Eds.). *Women, dissent, and anti-slavery in Britain and America, 1790–1865*. Oxford University Press.

University of Leicester. (2023). *Women's writing in the Midlands, 1750-1850*.

https://le.ac.uk/new-writing/commissions/womens-writing-midlands

Vaux, T. (1983). Delaware Valley women's history: An overview. In T. Vaux (Ed.). *Guide to women's history resources in the Delaware Valley area*. University of Pennsylvania Press.

Walters, K. (2020). *Harriet Tubman: A life in American history*. ABC-CLIO.

Washington, M. (2009). *Sojourner Truth's America*. University of Illinois Press.

Wayne, T.K. (Ed.). (2020). *Women's suffrage: The complete guide to the Nineteenth Amendment*. ABC-CLIO.

Whalin, W.T. (1997). *Sojourner Truth*. Barbour Publishing, Inc.

Whipps, J. (2023). *Sarah Grimké (1792–1873) and Angelina Grimké Weld (1805–1879)*. Internet Encyclopedia of Philosophy. https://iep.utm.edu/Grimké/

White, D.G., Bay, M., & Martin, W.E. (2013). *Freedom in my mind: A history of African Americans*. Bedford/St. Martins.

Williams, G.W. (2022). *The history of black people in America from 1619 to 1880*. E-artnow.

Williamson, S.C. (2002). *The narrative life: The moral and religious thought of Frederick Douglass*. Mercer University Press.

Wilson, E.G. (1989). *Thomas Clarkson: A biography*. Macmillan.

Wilson, T.D. (2012). *The Oglethorpe plan: Enlightenment

design in Savannah and beyond. University of Virginia Press.

Wise, S.M. (2005). *Through the heavens may fall: The landmark trial that led to the end of human slavery*. Da Capo Press.

Women and the American Story. (2023a). *Life story: The Grimké sisters*. New-York Historical Society. https://wams.nyhistory.org/a-nation-divided/antebellum/Grimké-sisters/

Women and the American Story. (2023b).
Life story: Mary Ann Shadd Cary (1823–1893).
https://wams.nyhistory.org/expansions-and-inequalities/politics-and-society/mary-ann-shadd-cary/

Yarhi, E. (2023). *Mary Ann Shadd: American educator, publisher, and abolitionist*. Britannica.com. https://www.britannica.com/biography/Mary-Ann-Shadd-Cary

Yasumura, G. Contemporary Monuments to the Slave Past, (2023). *Sojourner Truth monuments. Contemporary Monuments to the Slave Past.* https://www.slaverymonuments.org/collections/show/9

Yee, S.J. (1997). Finding a place: Mary Ann Shadd Cary and the dilemmas of black migration to Canada, 1850–1870. *Frontiers: A Journal of Women Studies, 18*(3): 1–16.

Zoellner, T. (2020). *How one woman pulled off the first consumer boycott–and helped inspire the British to abolish slavery*. The Conversation. https://theconversation.com/how-one-woman-pulled-off-the-first-consumer-boycott-and-helped-inspire-the-british-to-abolish-slavery-140313

www.ingramcontent.com/pod-product-compliance
Lightning Source LLC
Chambersburg PA
CBHW031115080526
44587CB00011B/977